THE
STEVE
JOBS
WAY

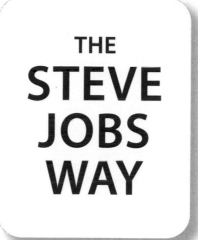

THE
STEVE
JOBS
WAY

iLEADERSHIP
FOR A
NEW GENERATION

Jay Elliot

FORMER SENIOR VICE PRESIDENT, APPLE COMPUTER

WITH **William L. Simon**

 Vanguard Press
A Member of the Perseus Books Group

Poster on page 39: Stéphane Massa-Bidal / Retrofuturs:
http://www.retrofuturs.com

Published by Vanguard Press
A Member of the Perseus Books Group

Set in 11 point Dante MT

Library of Congress Cataloging-in-Publication Data

Elliot, Jay.
    The Steve Jobs way : iLeadership for a new generation / Jay Elliot with
William L. Simon.
        p. cm.
    Includes bibliographical references.
    ISBN 978-1-59315-639-8 (hardcover : alk. paper)
    ISBN 978-1-59315-664-0 (e-book)
    1. Jobs, Steven, 1955– 2. Computer engineers—United States—Biography.
3. Businesspeople—United States—Biography. 4. Apple Computer, Inc.—
History. 5. Computer industry—United States—History. I. Simon, William L.,
1930– II. Title.
QA76.2.J63E45 2011
621.39092—dc22
[B]
                                                            2010049400

10 9 8 7 6 5 4 3 2 1

For my wife Liliana,
and my sons Jay-Alexander
and Federico for their loving support

And for Arynne, Victoria, and Charlotte,
and Sheldon, Vincent, and Elena

Contents

Author's Note

Sometimes Things Happen . . .

. . . that turn out so well we couldn't have improved on them if we'd mapped out our own lives in advance.

Of course, what are called the "glamour" jobs—the movies, television, the music business, fashion—often only seem glamorous from the outside: Working in one of those fields is fraught with constant challenges and frustrations.

Hardly anyone thinks of technology as a glamour field, but for me, at least, work has never been as satisfying or as unbelievably exciting as when I was working with Steve Jobs.

Because it's awkward to write "products and services" throughout, I have instead used just "product"—counting on you to understand that the term is intended to include services, as well.

I've known and worked with the leaders of IBM and Intel; I've met great leaders and thinkers, including Jack Welch, Buckminster Fuller, and Joseph Campbell, and discussed the next paradigm change in organizational structure with John Drucker.

Steve is in a class by himself.

The major business journals often disagree, yet there is a consensus that Steve Jobs is the leader of the most outstanding company in the history of business. Steve does seemingly impossible things, every day.

So what is it that has made Steve so unique in the ways he runs an organization that brings such convenience, time-saving, and pleasure to so many people around the world? That's the question I have set out to answer here.

This is not only about how you shift your paradigm, but how you get your organization to shift with you. The principles of "iLeadership" presented here offer the key elements involving the product or service you offer, the people and teams, the organization itself, and the innovation engine to connect what you do and what you make with the customers you are trying to reach. Steve Jobs provides probably the best example possible of how a leader can implement these changes and run even a very large organization as if it were in start-up mode.

Some of the advice I give will not seem easy or comfortable. I will ask you to think in ways that you are not used to. But you can improve your business and your life if you are courageous enough to carry out the iLeadership principles you will find in these pages.

Jay Elliot

Prologue

I was sitting in the waiting area of a restaurant . . .

. . . which has to be one of the most unlikely places in the world for an encounter that changes your life.

The headline story I was reading in the business section told about the calamitous end of start-up Eagle Computer. A young man who was also waiting was reading the same article. We fell into conversation and I shared my connection with that story. I had just recently told my boss, Intel president Andy Grove, that I would be quitting my position at his company to join the guys who were starting Eagle Computer. The company was just about to go public.

The day of the public offering, the CEO became an instant multi-millionaire and celebrated by going out drinking with his cofounders. From there he drove right over to buy himself a Ferrari, took a car from the dealership for a happy test drive, and crashed. He died, the company died, and the job I had quit Intel to take was over before I had even reported for work.

The young man I had told this story to started asking questions about my background. We were quite a contrast: He was this hippie-looking twenty-something in jeans and sneakers. In me he saw a six-foot-five athlete in his forties, a corporate type in suit and tie. About the only thing we seemed to have in common was that at the time we were both wearing beards.

But we quickly discovered a shared passion for computers. The guy was a fire-eater, bursting with energy, lighting up at the idea that I had held key positions in technology but had left IBM when I found them slow to accept new ideas.

He introduced himself as Steve Jobs, Board Chairman of Apple Computer. I had barely heard of Apple, but I had trouble seeing this youngster as head of a computer company.

Then he took me entirely by surprise, saying he'd like me to come work for him. I answered, "I don't think you can afford me." At the time, Steve was twenty-five and later that same year, when Apple went public, would be worth something like $250 million. He, and the company, could afford me.

On a Friday two weeks later, I started working for Apple—at a slightly higher salary and with many more stock options than I had had at Intel, and with a parting message from Andy Grove that I was "making a big mistake—Apple isn't going anywhere."

Steve likes to surprise people by not sharing information until the last minute, maybe as a way of keeping you a little bit off balance and a little more under his control. My very first day on the job, at the end of an afternoon get-to-know-each-other-better chat, he said, "Let's take a ride tomorrow. Meet me here at ten. I want to show you something." I had no idea what to expect or whether I should be preparing myself in some way.

Saturday morning we got into Steve's Mercedes and drove off. Music was blaring out of the car's speakers: the Police and the Beatles, uncomfortably loud. Still no word of where we were heading.

He pulled into the parking lot at PARC, the Xerox Palo Alto Research Center, where we were ushered into a room of computer equipment that blew me away. Steve had been there a month earlier with a group of Apple engineers, who had been divided about whether the goodies they had seen would amount to anything of value for personal computers.

Now Steve was back for another look, and he was on fire. His voice changes when he sees something "insanely great," and I witnessed it that day. We saw a crude version of a device we'd later call a mouse, a computer printer, and a computer display that wasn't limited to text and numbers but could show drawings and graphic images, and menu items you could select with the mouse. Steve talked afterward about those PARC visits as "apocalyptic." He was sure he had seen the future of computing.

PARC was creating a machine for the enterprise, a mainframe computer to compete with IBM, expected to carry a price tag of $10,000 to $20,000. Steve had seen something else: a computer for everyone.

But he hadn't just seen computer technology. Like a boy in Middle-Ages Italy who entered a monastery and discovered Jesus, Steve had just discovered the religion of "user-friendly." Or maybe he had already had the lust and had just now discovered that there was a way to satisfy it. Steve the ultimate consumer, Steve the envisioner of product perfection, had stumbled upon the shining path to a glowing future.

Sure, it wasn't going to be a smooth path. He would make a lot of grievous, costly, near-disastrous mistakes along the way—many of them because of a sense of his own infallibility, the kind of stubborn certainty that gave rise to the cliché, "my way or the highway."

But for me, his newly acquired sidekick, it was awesome to see how open he was to possibilities, how excited he was about recognizing new ideas, seeing their value, and embracing them. And his enthusiasm is infectious. He understands the mind-set of the people he wants to create products for because he is one of them. And because he thinks like his future customers, he knows when he has seen the future.

I would come to see Steve as incredibly bright, overflowing with enthusiasm, driven by a vision of the future, but also incredibly young and wildly impulsive. How did he see me? As something I believe he had been looking for and hadn't yet found. In me, he finally had a senior guy who had a solid grounding in business. Though my new title was senior vice president of Apple Computer, Inc., the job came with unofficial duties as Steve's sidekick, mentor, and graybeard (I was forty-four years old). Before long he would be telling people, "Don't trust anyone over forty except Jay."

Though Steve was no techie, he burned to have a product of his own. He had been out drumming up sales and making deals while Woz was creating the company's first computers, yet he ached to prove his insights by creating a machine that would bear his own imprint. When he tried to press his vision of the future on the engineers designing Apple's Lisa computer, just to get rid of him the Lisa engineers kept saying things like, "If you think those ideas are so good, go build your own computer."

No, Steve didn't have a crystal ball that told him he'd be creating one hot, stunning product after another. And he was never introspective enough to stop and ponder how it had all come about. You might say that he earned credibility without even noticing.

But at the time, for me, it was awesome to see how open he was to new possibilities, how excited about seeing new thinking, recognizing its value, and embracing it.

Steve's eye-opening experiences at PARC were to become some of the most famous, most written-about events in the history of technology. From those visits, Steve Jobs would set out to change the world.

And that, of course, is exactly what he did.

PART I

PRODUCT CZAR

1

Passion for the Product

Some people choose their path in life. Some people have it thrust on them. And then there are some who discover their calling almost by accident, never having looked for it.

Steven Paul Jobs didn't set out to be a Product Czar. If I had called him that in the early days, I'm not sure he would have known what I was talking about. He might even have laughed at me.

Okay, I'm not going to claim I recognized it at the time. No one did. Certainly not Paul and Clara Jobs, the devoted couple who had suffered through his early school years when he was so unruly and hard to handle that, as he says himself, he could well have been headed for jail.

So to see him become the world's foremost CEO and product creator is all the more unlikely and impressive. Yet the man I saw when I first went to work with him certainly was determined and driven. And like all the great leaders I'd met and worked with, he had his own personal, nearly irrational focus—but it's one that has made the world a better place. His obsession is *a passion for the product . . . a passion for product perfection.*

What shape does that obsession take? Easy. Steve is *the world's greatest consumer.* I saw it from the day I joined Apple. He breathed life into the Macintosh as "the computer for the rest of us." He stirred the iTunes Store and the iPod into being out of his love for music and the desire to take music everywhere with him. He loved the convenience of the cell phone but hated the heavy, clumsy, ugly, hard-to-use phones on the market, and that dissatisfaction led to his giving himself and the rest of us the iPhone.

Steve Jobs survives, thrives, and changes society by following his own passions.

I got my first whiff of his passions on that visit to PARC. The rest of that weekend, I kept reliving the experience. Every detail of those two hours kept running through my mind, and I recognized that what I had seen was something extraordinary. Steve had been full of excitement, off the scale with unbounded enthusiasm. This was passion in its most raw form, the passion for an idea. For Steve, it was already shaping into a passion for a specific product.

From everything he had said to me while we were there and on the way home, two things were obvious: Steve was a man who even then had a vision about the power of the computer to change people's lives. And he knew that he had come face to face with the concepts that were going to make that possible. In particular he had been blown away by the notion of an icon on the screen—a cursor—that was controlled by the movement of your hand. Steve saw that in a nanosecond, capturing a vision of the future of computing.

It wasn't just the technology at PARC that had so impressed Steve, it was the people as well. And the admiration flowed in both directions. PARC scientist Larry Tessler several years later would tell journalist and author Jeffrey Young about his recollection of Steve's visit with the team from Apple. "What impressed me was that their questions were better than any I had heard in the seven years I had been at Xerox. From anybody—Xerox employee, visitor, university professor, student. Their questions showed that they understood all the implications, and they understood the subtleties, too. Nobody else who had ever seen the demo cared as much about the subtleties. Why the patterns were there in the title of the window. Why the pop-up menus looked the way they did."

Tessler was so impressed that he would soon leave PARC to join Apple, with the title of vice president, at the same time becoming Apple's first chief scientist.

In my ten years at IBM, I had rubbed shoulders with too many brilliant PhD scientists who were doing exceptional work yet were frustrated because so few of their contributions were adopted and made into products. At PARC, I had smelled the rancid odor of frustration in the air, so it wasn't surprising to learn that they had a 25 percent turnover rate, one of the highest in the industry.

At the time I joined Apple, the heat at the company was being generated by a development group working on what was supposed to be a boundary-shattering product, a computer that would come to be called the Lisa. It was meant to serve as a complete break from Apple II technology and launch the company in a completely new direction, using some of the same innovations the Apple engineers had seen at PARC. Steve told me the Lisa would be such a breakthrough that "it will make a dent in the universe." You couldn't help but be in awe of talk like that; the line has been an inspiration for me ever since, a reminder that you won't get people working for you fired up with enthusiasm unless you're fired up yourself . . . and you let everyone know it.

The Lisa had been in development for two years, but no matter. The technology Steve had seen at PARC was going to change the world, and the Lisa would have to be completely rethought along the new lines. He tried to get the Lisa team turned on about what he had seen at PARC.

"You've gotta change direction," he kept insisting. The engineers and programmers of the Lisa were Woz worshippers and not about to be redirected by Steve Jobs.

Apple in those days was something of a runaway ship, plowing through the water at full speed with lots of people on the bridge but no one really in command. The company, though barely four years old, was enjoying annual net sales of around $300 million. Steve was co-founder but no longer had the clout of the early days when it was just the two Steves, with Woz tending to the technology and SJ taking care of everything else. The CEO had left, start-up-investor Mike Markkula was acting as interim CEO, with Michael Scott ("Scotty") as president, both of them more than competent but neither qualified to run a bustling technology company. Mike, the second-largest shareholder was more interested, I thought, in retiring than in the daily hassles of a rapidly growing technology business. The two decision-makers didn't want the delays in getting the Lisa to market that Steve's changes would mean. The project was behind schedule already, and the idea of throwing out what had been done and starting down a new path simply wasn't acceptable.

To ram his demands down the throats of the Lisa team or the guys running the company, Steve had a scenario laid out in his head: He would be slotted as vice president of new product development, which would make him supreme commander over the Lisa team with the muscle to command the change in direction he had been trying to press on them.

Instead, in an organizational reshuffling, Markkula and Scott had given Steve the title of board chairman, explaining that this would make him the company's front man for the upcoming initial public offering of Apple stock; to have the charismatic twenty-five-year-old as the Apple spokesman would help boost the stock price and make him all the richer, they argued.

Steve was really hurt. He was unhappy about the way Scotty had pulled this stunt without informing or consulting him—it was his company, after all! And he was really upset about losing direct involvement with the Lisa. He was just really bent out of shape.

The sting was even worse. The new head of the Lisa group, John Couch, told Steve to stop coming around and harassing his engineers; he was to stay away and leave them alone.

Steve Jobs doesn't hear the word "no" and is deaf to "We can't" or "You may not."

What do you do if you have in your head a continent-shifting product but your company doesn't take any interest? I saw Steve become very focused at that point. Instead of acting like a child whose toys had been snatched away, he became disciplined and determined.

He had never found himself in a position like this before, being told "Hands off" within his own company; few people ever have. On one hand, he took me along to board meetings where I saw him running those sessions as a board chairman more knowledgeable than the older, wiser, vastly more experienced CEOs who were sitting around the table. He had in his head volumes of current data about Apple's financial position, margins, cash flow, the Apple II sales in various market segments and sales regions, and other business minutia. Today everybody thinks of him as an incredible technologist, a product-creator extraordinaire, but he's much more, and has been from the very beginning.

Yet on the other hand, his role as an idea-person and shaper of new products had just been snatched away from him. Steve had a clear vision of the future of computing sledgehammering his brain, but nowhere to go with it. The doors to the Lisa group had been slammed in his face and locked tight against him.

What now?

• • •

This was at a time when Apple was flush with money, millions of dollars in the bank from the booming sales of the Apple II. The cash made possible little innovative projects springing up everywhere in the company. It was just the kind of spirit any company would benefit from, when the attitude was to try to create a brave new world by dreaming up something brand-new, something never done before.

From my first week there, I had been sensing the passion and drive that had everyone charged up. I had this image of two engineers meeting in the hallway, one of them describing an idea he had been toying with, his buddy saying something like, "That's great, you should do something with it," and the first one going back to his lab, pulling a team together, and spending months developing the idea. I'd be willing to bet that was happening all over the company in those days. Most of the projects would never go anywhere, would never earn a penny of revenue, and some were duplicating what another group was also working on. But it didn't matter; enough would be successful to make a difference. The company was fat with cash, and bustling with creative ideas.

There was one particular early-stage development project at Apple, a project Steve had not long before tried to kill because, he said, it would be in competition with the Lisa. Now he went back to see how the project team was doing. He found the handful of people at work in a building everyone referred to as "Texaco Towers" because it was near a Texaco gas station. Dedicated to creating an easy-to-use, inexpensive computer for the masses, the team had been at work only a few months but had already developed a working prototype. And their computer already had a name: Taking a leaf from the name of the company, the new machine had been dubbed "Macintosh." (The head of the team, a brilliant former professor named Jef Raskin, chose the name of his favorite brand of apple; it would become part of Apple lore that he meant to use the same spelling as the apple—*McIntosh*—but got the spelling wrong, though Raskin later insisted he had intentionally used a different spelling to avoid confusion.)

Steve no longer wanted to cancel the project. If the Lisa team didn't want to listen to his evangelism for a new kind of computing, the small Macintosh team had hackers who thought like Steve and might be more open to his ideas.

When the company's cofounder, board chairman, and poster boy for high-tech started frequent visits to the Macintosh work group, the team turned out to have a mixed reaction. They felt inspired by Steve's passion and commitment but at the same time, in the words one team member put into a memo, found that he "seems to introduce tension, politics, and hassles." Right: High achievers and people with a vision are sometimes short on social skills, or just don't care about politeness or being tactful.

They didn't have a choice. Steve simply took over the team and began adding new people, calling meetings, setting new directions. Steve's major beef with team-leader Raskin centered on how the user would give instructions to the computer. Jef wanted commands to be given with the keyboard; Steve knew there was a better way: moving the cursor with some kind of control device. He ordered the Macintosh team to explore the best ways to control the cursor, and the best ways to use the cursor for giving the command to, say, open a file or display a list of options. The fundamentals of the way we use computers today—moving the cursor with the mouse, clicking to make a selection, dragging a file or icon, and all the rest—were ideas fleshed out from PARC and nurtured by the team through Steve's relentless insistence on simplicity, elegance of design, and intuitiveness.

Besides my duties at the corporate level, Steve also wanted me as a sounding board, a kind of mentor and advisor, especially on the business and organizational issues. So he gave me a second role, on the Macintosh team. I was to be an advisor-without-title, a full-fledged team member with no official status. Steve and I met almost daily, or took walks around Bandley Drive. He used me to bounce ideas off and to get a second opinion on issues about people, projects, marketing, sales—just about everything. We would have long discussions on how to make the Mac group the new paradigm for Corporate America.

He saw me as a partner in helping make his dream happen: a self-made person with a breadth of business experience in two leading technology companies. I think he also saw me as easygoing, a balance to himself. And I was a peacemaker. Steve's assistant, Pat Sharp, would sometimes tell people, "When Jay walks into the room, Steve becomes a different person." She meant he'd calm down.

The qualities that Steve recognized in me came from my rather unusual background. My father was what most people would call a farmer but to us was a "rancher." The homestead was the Año Nuevo ("New Year") ranch: 1,000 acres along the Monterey coast of northern California, with three and a half miles of shoreline and two inland lakes large enough for small sailboats. The area had been discovered by Father Junipero Sierra in 1775. My mother's family were pioneers who had come west in covered wagons and settled on the land in the late 1800s, when California was a new state. (Today we have turned over most of Año Nuevo to the state and it has become the visiting place for thousands of tourists a year to see the elephant seals.)

One of my great-great-grandfathers, Frederick Steele, had been the West Point roommate of Ulysses S. Grant and had served as Grant's right-hand man in the Civil War. I still own a family heirloom, the document making Steele a general, signed by Abraham Lincoln.

Crops and livestock wait for no man. The family was up at five every day, even on weekends, and I wouldn't see my dad until we sat down together for dinner at six—parents, grandmother, two sisters, sometimes my brother and his wife, plus our ramrod farm manager.

Farm kids work long hours, as well—school, homework, and farm chores. The cows get milked at five in the morning and five in the evening, weekdays and weekends, in sun, darkness, fog, or thunderstorm. Once you're old enough to drive a tractor, you better know how to repair it, too; when it breaks down twenty miles from the barn, it's a long walk for help if you aren't a do-it-yourself fix-it guy (though surely less of an issue today, thanks to the cell phone).

It's not an easy life but it teaches you independence. If you weren't creative, there was nothing much in the way of entertainment. I made my own surfboards and crafted two sailboats that actually sailed pretty well. Then when I was fifteen, my father announced that he would focus on his duties with the school board and other civic responsibilities for the coming year, and would leave me in charge of running the farm. I still don't know what made him think I could possibly do it.

I wanted to make a difference. On a large ranch, generally one bumper crop in five years is enough to keep you going. I wanted to create that bumper crop . . . but of what? What could I plant? You have to plan six months ahead, guessing what the price level will be at harvest time. I discovered a fascination with the Farmers' Almanac, a most incredible document. Based on the Almanac's weather predictions for the growing season, and the advice from area berry growers, I decided to put in strawberries, and brought in a Japanese family who knew the crop.

It turned out to be a fantastically profitable year—for the ranch, and for me. I believe the experience gave me confidence in myself and a sense that I could accomplish more than I might have thought possible.

Something else I learned from farming. Maybe each ranch is different, but Año Nuevo was no top-down, do-as-I-say operation. If you saw something wrong, you spoke up about it. That attitude became core to my personality and on my first job in the business world, at IBM, led me to a step I guess not very many people would have taken. The company's president, Tom Watson, Jr., son of IBM's first president, testified before the Senate Foreign Relations Committee as they looked for answers about what had gone wrong in Vietnam. He said the problem had been the logistics of fighting the war.

That attitude from my ranch childhood of speaking up when you see something you think is wrong tugged at me when I read in the newspaper about Watson's testimony. I sat down and drafted a carefully reasoned letter saying that I thought IBM was making the same kind of mistake. I admired the respect that the company showed for its employees and its corporate customers, but I thought they were missing a major opportunity by not becoming a force in the consumer market.

I got a call from Watson's aide saying that Mr. Watson was going to be visiting the IBM facility where I worked the following week and would like me to meet with him. I walked in nervous as hell, certain it was my last day with the company. Instead he said he was impressed with my insight, appreciated that I would speak up, and he would consider my suggestions. From then on, whenever he was at an IBM facility where I was working, Tom Watson would arrange to visit with me for another chat.

I think my business experience at IBM and later at Intel, combined with an easygoing way and the ability to make suggestions and offer opinions without rancor, were qualities that worked for me with Steve Jobs.

Apple had sprung to life with two computers that were the brainwork of the company's cofounder, Steve Wozniak (known universally as Woz, though he prefers to be called Steve). Woz's path to fame is as intriguing as that of his ultimate partner. In a 1996 interview, he told author/journalist Jill Wolfson that he had been influenced at a young age by the Tom Swift books about "this young guy who was an engineer who could design anything, and he owned his own company, and he would entrap aliens, and build submarines, and have projects all over the world." Woz was so enthralled that to him it was "like the first TV shows you ever watched." Inspired, he began doing science fair projects so elaborate that by sixth grade, he created a computer-like machine that played tic-tac-toe.

He continued on the same path through high school and college, teaching himself about computers by doing continually more advanced tasks until he was eventually designing and building complete computers.

Asked how he would summarize his life in one word, he answered without hesitation: "Lucky. Every dream I've ever had in life has come true ten times over." He told the interviewer that, though never a church-goer, from childhood he embraced a set of values that he feels were Christian-like. "If somebody does something bad to you, you don't fight back. You're still good to them and treat them with love from your heart."

Woz also revealed a degree of modesty that is absent in his co-founder. "I wonder why, when I just did . . . some good engineering, . . . some people think that I'm some kind of hero or a special person. But it's really the body of people and their mass thinking that caused computers to happen."

Yet for all his contributions to launching the computer revolution, Steve has That's Woz all the way—sharing credit.

Steve Jobs didn't have as much technical knowledge or ability as Woz had in his little finger. So how did he come to master the intricacies of computer technology?

He told me once that he discovered a fascination with computers early, in his preteen years, on a visit to the NASA Ames Research Center in nearby Mountain View. Actually, it turned out that he didn't really see the computer itself; all he saw was the terminal. When he talks about it, you can still see the boyish enthusiasm, and you can hear it when he says that he "fell in love" with the whole idea of computers that day.

Talking about those early days for the PBS documentary *Triumph of the Nerds*, he shed some light on this: "You would keyboard these commands in and then you would wait for a while and then the thing would go dadadadadada and it would tell you something out but even with that it was still remarkable, especially for a ten year old, that you could write a program in Basic let's say or Fortran and actually this machine would . . . take your idea and it would . . . execute your idea and give you back some results. And if they were the results that you predicted, your program really worked. It was an incredibly thrilling experience."

You don't become a leading technology worker without first spending intensive years in the classroom. But that firm rule of life somehow didn't apply to Steve Jobs. I was witness to a phenomenon that was almost unbelievable. Here was a young man who had dropped out of college after little more than a semester, taken himself off to India where he traveled not like a tourist but more like an itinerant beggar-monk, and had become absorbed with Buddhism, which became a lifelong commitment. (On a train trip with him in Japan once, he pointed out to me a Buddhist temple we were passing, explaining that after his journey through India, he had decided he would go to live at this temple and become a Buddhist priest. And would have, he said, except for that little project he started with the neighborhood kid Steve Wozniak. Amazing how our lives sometimes take a different course than we could possibly have expected.)

Now, instead of a neophyte monk, Steve Jobs was turning into an incredibly astute technowizard.

He quickly became a master of every aspect of the Macintosh design, system architecture, and functionality. His grasp of the technology was so deep that he could discuss with each of the engineers the details of what he was working on—wanting to know what the progress was, why the engineer had made this decision instead of that one, deciding that some choice wasn't the best and ordering a change. Even something as fundamental as what computer chip would drive the Macintosh: Steve ordered the team to create a whole new prototype of the computer using a different chip, the Motorola 68000, which featured a larger memory. They grumbled but obeyed; it proved to be the right decision.

Once when Mac engineer Trip Hawkins was interviewed about his time at Apple, he described Steve as having "a power of vision that is almost frightening. When Steve believes in something, the power of that vision can literally sweep aside any objections, problems or whatever. They just cease to exist."

What made Steve Jobs tick? In my role as what I might call his left-hand man (because he's left-handed), I found the answer expressed in comments he made in conversations about himself and his way of seeing his role and goal. Great products only come from people who are passionate. Great products only come from *teams* that are passionate.

The vision Trip Hawkins talked about came from Steve's focus, but even more from his passion. I loved what Steve would say about this, setting a standard for himself and everyone around him of doing each task the very best you can "because you only get to do a limited number of things in your life." Like any passionate artist, he has always been driven by his passion for his creations, his products. The Mac and every product since are more than "just products." They are a representation of Steve Jobs's intense commitment. Visionaries are able to create great art or great products because their work isn't nine-to-five. What Steve was doing represented him; it was intuitive but inspired. He didn't know he was doing something Einstein had recommended: "Follow what's mysterious." Yet it would not be until years after the first Macintosh, much water under the bridge, and some embarrassing missteps that Steve would come to recognize that his true passion wasn't simply to create great products, but was something more specific, more focused—as we shall see later in these pages. It would lead him to the series of elegant, accessible, intuitive, beautiful, powerful devices that have come to define his career. The whole world would change for him . . . and he would change the world.

"I could be doing a lot of other things with my life," he said. "But the Macintosh is going to change the world. I believe that, and I've chosen people for the team who believe it, too."

This product passion goes through the entire Apple organization—from the receptionists to the engineers to the members of the board of directors. If the employees of any company do not feel this passion as passed on from the leaders, than the leaders need to be asking, "Why not?"

As his own product czar, Steve wore a dazzling number of different hats in the Macintosh team, starting with product conceiver-in-chief. From the drawing board to delivery, he *inhabited* the product, living every detail of what it would experience, as if it were a living, breathing organism.

He knew he had to be surrounded by people as invested in achieving excellence in the products as he himself was. His passion is one of the great underlying secrets of Steve's success. He is exacting, and demanding, and, yes, at times inconsiderate. It's all a reflection of the fiery passion that drives him.

Most people, Steve believes, don't have what it takes to be an entrepreneur or product manager. He talked about this when he was trying to make a go of NeXT. "A lot of people," he said, "come to me and say 'I want to be an entrepreneur.'" When he asks them, "What's your idea?" they say, "I don't have one yet."

He tells people like this, "I think you should go get a job as a busboy or something until you find something you're really passionate about."

He believes that "about half of what separates the successful entrepreneurs from the non-successful ones is pure perseverance.

"You put so much of your life into this thing. There are such rough moments in time that I think most people give up. I don't blame them. It's really tough and it consumes your life."

You have to be burning with "an idea, or a problem, or a wrong that you want to right." If you're not passionate enough from the start, you'll never stick it out.

2

Success Is
in the Details

Steve Jobs understood something that a lot of companies try to do, but are rarely successful at. The more he advanced, the simpler his products became. In some instances, it's less about the product and more about the user. Every user wants to feel successful. When you know how to operate something masterfully, how does it make you feel? More people will buy if customers feel good using the product.

For Steve, nothing is wasted, nothing is unnecessary. It doesn't happen by cramming in more, it happens through creativity and innovation, with a relentless pursuit of perfection. It means thinking through everything with the laser-focused goal of making it intuitive to the user. The irony is that this takes more work, more detail-oriented planning.

You probably know a few people—or perhaps more than a few—who consider themselves "detail oriented." Maybe you'd even put yourself in that category. Steve's level of focus on details is one of the most crucial aspects of his success and the success of his products.

• • •

He wore a Porsche wristwatch, again chosen because he was so in awe of the museum-quality design. Whenever anyone noticed the watch and admired it, Steve would take it off his wrist and present it as a gift, a way of saying, "Congratulations on recognizing excellent design." Minutes later, he would have an identical one on his wrist again: He kept a box of them in this office so he could give them away . . . at around $2,000 apiece.

(The band on the one he gave me broke a couple of years ago; because the band was integrated into the body and both were made of titanium, it couldn't be fixed. I never asked Steve if those watches were his inspiration for the titanium Mac.)

Looking back, I see those parking-lot sessions and wristwatch fixations as symbolic of what was to become an essential feature of the Jobsian character and of Steve's success as a crafter of products: his willingness—or maybe I should say his absolute, fundamental need—to focus in on a single aspect or detail, clearing everything from his vision and his mind until he arrived at the decision he was looking for.

Sure, we all focus our attention now and then. Steve, though, treats every aspect of a product or decision to the same intense level of scrutiny. He first applies his vision to where he wants to go, then to the vision of the product—how it will work, how it will fit into the natural ways of life, how people use things.

Anticipating the User Experience

Steve wanted to live every detail of the experience. When you're at home or in your office with your new computer, what will you see when you first open the box? How many things do you have to remove before you can lift out the computer, and how convenient are they to get to? He'd say to the development team, "Okay, I'm the product. What's happening to me when the buyer tries to take me out of the box and start me up?" He was always discovering imperfections in everything, from the design, to the user experience and user-interface, to the marketing and packaging, to how the product would be marketed and sold.

I was awed by these performances. This was passion for the details at its finest—passion combined with courage in his own vision and his confidence as the ultimate consumer.

The mouse would be brand-new to users: How could the packaging be designed so that you get the tactile sensation of holding the mouse in your hand from the first moment you take it out of the box?

How can the case of the computer be designed so it looks handsome— something that pleases the eye and you're proud to have on your desk? Not just an ugly cabinet with square corners, looking like it was designed by an engineer.

How quickly can the Macintosh come on when you plug it in and first press the power switch?

What will you see when the screen comes to life each time you turn it on?

Will you be able to figure out how to do all the basic operations *without looking at a user manual?*

In a meeting with the people writing the Macintosh support documentation, someone threw into the conversation the common wisdom of the day: that the user manual should be written at the twelfth-grade level. Steve did not take the suggestion kindly. "No," he said. "At the *first*-grade level." He said it was one of his dreams that the Mac would be so simple to use there wouldn't be any need for a manual.

And then he added, "Maybe we should get a first-grader to write it!"

He knew there would have to be functions that couldn't be made intuitive; he accepted that only the simplest of devices could be completely intuitive, but he also knew that if his designers and programmers struggled hard enough, they could come up with brilliant ways of making the Mac (and everything that followed) easy to use.

For Steve, success is in the details.

Simplicity

Forever determined to make every product as simple and uncomplicated as possible, Steve got a kick out of a story I shared with him once, about how much I admired the 1932 Ford Model A. As a reward for working hard at the ranch, I was given an old Model A as the big present on my fifteenth birthday. I needed to do a lot of work on the engine, brakes, and body—it was then already over twenty years old. But Henry Ford's people had done such a good job that it was very easy, without a manual, to work on the engine. Ford had thought it out in such detail that at the factory, the wood slats from the packing case the parts came in were used as structure pieces for the floorboards, seats, and interior of the car. And if you had to replace them, the type and size of the wood was etched into the back so you'd know what to look for. Telling Steve this story, I pointed out that when the car was introduced, its competition was a horse and there were no repair stations yet.

Computer buyers had never seen a mouse before: Its competition was the keyboard. It made me think of what Henry Ford had done—those early drivers had to learn to use clutch, accelerator, and gearshift to get going. The mouse was just as novel to the user, but would take a great deal less learning.

When Steve Jobs had his best engineers working on the top-secret project to develop the iPhone, he had to wage a battle. Trying to create a cell phone product was a monumental effort for a company with no background in the field. One of his big reasons for taking on this unlikely challenge was that every cell phone he had ever seen was in his view far too complicated to use: a perfect challenge for a man so dedicated to detail and to its companion quality, simplicity.

So Steve had decided early on that the cell phone being developed at Apple would have only a *single* button.

His engineers kept telling him over and over in their once-or-twice-a-week review meetings that it was not possible for a cell phone to have only one button. You could not turn it on and off, control the volume, switch between functions, go on the Internet, and use all the other features the phone was to have, if you had only a single control button.

Steve was deaf to their complaints. He kept demanding in effect, "The phone will have only one button. Figure it out."

Though he has through the years been an incredible solver of problems and originator of clever idea on all of the products developed under him, Steve didn't know how the phone could be designed so it would need only one button. But as the ultimate consumer, he knew that's what he wanted. He kept sending the engineers back with the demand that they figure out the necessary solutions.

You know the end of the story: The original iPhone had only one control button.

Hand Out

Steve was fascinated with the amazing abilities of the human hand, simply intrigued by the hand and how it works with the arm.

Sometimes in a meeting I'd notice him hold one hand up in front of his face and turn it slowly, looking totally absorbed with how the hand is configured and what it's capable of doing. For ten or fifteen seconds at a time, he would seem completely zoned out on this exercise. You only had to see him do that once or twice to understand what it meant: The fingers could be vastly more useful for relaying instructions to the computer than just pecking at keys on a keyboard.

Following up on his insight from the PARC visits, he would often talk about how the hands are this incredible device, and he'd say things like, "The hand is the most used part of your body to implement what your brain wants." And, "If you could only replicate the hand, that would be a killer product." In hindsight, this was an incredibly powerful observation of a detail that has lead to the current cast of Apple products, from the Mac, to the iPod, iPhone, and iPad.

Steve had the Mac team try a variety of input devices for controlling the cursor; one was pen-like, and I think another was like a tablet, more or less like today's laptop touchpad. It took a while until he was convinced that nothing else worked as well as the mouse. Everything from drop-down menus to editing commands like cut-and-paste were made possible because of the ability to move the cursor.

The Ultimate User:
The Customer as Me, Me as the Customer

At the most fundamental level, the vision behind Apple products has to do with how Steve feels about products: He sees them as a personal and intimate part of human life. As an enthusiast and perfectionist with the power to implement his visions, he designs products with a love for sophisticated technology but with a beautiful simplicity of function that makes them objects embraced by even the most casual and non-technical of consumers.

When Steve creates a product for himself, he believes he's taking every consumer into consideration; designing for himself, he's designing for Mr. T. C. Mits: The Celebrated Man In The Street. And the celebrated woman, as well.

In the early days especially, it sometimes seemed that everyone working on a Steve project had horror stories to share about Steve's level of concern with the decisions being made. On the first Mac, he was a walk-around manager in the extreme. It was a small enough team—not more than about a hundred people at its peak, and that included the business side, publications, marketing, and all the rest. But he would be at your desk or in your cubicle with alarming regularity, wanting to Monday-morning-quarterback just about every decision you had made since his last visit.

And if he said something like, "That's shit," you needed to know that it might very well not be a criticism but a Stevian request: "I don't understand that—explain it to me."

It took most of the Mac team a while to figure out that what seemed like meddling and time-wasting and super-over-controlling was really the involvement of a leader who wasn't just asking because he was way too involved in the details. No, these were the actions of a man who had a vision of the product he wanted to create, and was absolutely going to satisfy himself that every choice, every decision, was the best one for getting there.

Getting It Right

If Steve was driven to make every product the ultimate expression of simplicity and intuitive understanding for the consumer, it was always paired with an equal drive to create. He was driven to imbue his products with two qualities: In addition to being intuitive, every product should create an experience so satisfying that the user would feel an *emotional* attachment to it.

For Steve, launching a product on time isn't nearly as important as getting it right—as near to perfection for the user as possible. Over and over, he has blown the whistle, stopped the forward movement toward the goal line, and ordered his product team to fall back and regroup. He did not want to make a product like the IBM PC, which as far as he was concerned was most useful as a doorstop. Just about every reputation-making product since Steve's return to Apple—just about *every one*—has missed its target launch date because Steve made the tough call, so unpopular with stockholders of most companies, that the product wasn't yet ready for primetime.

Months after the launch date that Steve had originally set, people on the Mac team were still wearing T-shirts with "May 1984" printed on the sleeve—with no product yet on the market.

But he no longer gets bad press for missing a deadline: He simply doesn't announce a new product until shortly before it's released. He pays no attention to rumors and "word on the street." All the advance guessing just fans the flames of anticipation.

Calling on Talents and Interests We Never Thought We'd Use

What's your most unusual and unused talent, ability, or area of knowledge that you never expect to have much use for?

We all have them: those latent talents or ragtag pieces of acquired knowledge that we never expect to play a meaningful role in our lives. Steve had a number of these. One example: In his short stay at Reed College, he had stumbled on the subject of calligraphy. This was a young man who had been bitten at an early age by the technology bug; why on earth would such a rarefied field as calligraphy have appealed to him?

His fascination with shapes and form stretches from the configuration of letters in fonts like Garamond or Myriad to the incredibly appealing, near perfection of the design of the iPhone. (For a time when I first knew him, he signed his name in a handsome cursive script, all lower case.)

To Steve, the graphics interface he had seen at PARC was an invitation: It meant his Macintosh would not have to have the cruddy, boring, eyesore typeface that had been the standard since the days of the first computer monitors. With a graphics display along the lines of what they had at PARC, the Macintosh could have a wide selection of handsome, eye-pleasing fonts with variable width, in a range of sizes, plus bold, italics, underscore, superscripts for mathematical notation, and more variations that Steve himself could conceive.

Not for the last time, Steve had armed himself with a vision of the future. Like my own experience with the Model A, early experiences can have a magic-like power if we remain open to recalling them at key moments.

Details, Details

Some of the stories about Steve's level of concern for the smallest details may make you smile while at the same time establishing a measuring stick we can all use.

In 2002, when Steve was trying to convince wary music industry executives to make deals with him for selling their music online, he was in contact with Hilary Rosen, chief executive of the trade association for the industry: RIAA—the Recording Industry Association of America. In that role, she sat in on a meeting between Steve and a couple of the team members who were designing the website for the Apple iTunes Music Store, and had just come back with the *nth* revision to give Steve yet another look. She later described her awe and amusement: "Steve spent about twenty minutes back and forth with the engineers about the best place within a three-square-inch section to put *three words*. He was that focused on the details."

A *Time* writer had a similar experience. He was once allowed to sit in on a meeting at Pixar and was equally awed by Steve's attention to detail. Some marketing folks from Disney had come to share the promotion plans for the release of *Toy Story 2*, and Steve was squinting over the color-coded items of posters, trailers, billboards, release dates, promotions for the soundtrack album and for toys based on the movie's characters, and so on. Steve was asking pointed, minute questions about the schedule for the television ads, events at Disneyland and Disney

World, and which of the television news and interview shows the studio people would be aiming to line up.

Steve, according to the article, was so "deeply into this" that he was "perusing the timeline like a rabbi studying Talmud." The writer was clearly impressed. But for anybody who has ever worked with him, nothing about his questions was surprising. He is that detailed about *everything*.

One more example: Steve's concern for details sometimes has far greater impact than whether Disney will lead their Christmas promotional displays with Pooh Bear or Buzz Lightyear. On the iPhone, the design team had been through an almost obscene number of variations for the enclosure, some barely discernible slight adjustments, some radically different, some calling for the enclosure to be made from totally different materials. And then one weekend, with the launch only months away, Steve finally woke up to a painful truth: He simply was not satisfied with the enclosure he had chosen.

He drove to work the next day knowing his iPhone team—troops who had already been working impossible hours—would not be happy with him. That didn't matter. Steve is the Michelangelo of product creation: He'll keep adding brushstrokes to the canvas until he is certain he has it right.

It's what he sometimes calls "pushing the reset button." Park's Larry Tessler, who had by then become Apple's "chief scientist," once said he didn't really know the meaning of *charisma* until he met Steve Jobs. When you believe in your product and in your people as totally as Steve does, your people will stick with you.

Apple had one of the highest retention rates in Silicon Valley, and even higher for the product teams. Few people left because of the work hours or the working conditions.

But the Apple troops know by now what to expect. When Steve says, "It's not right, we've got to trash this, take ten steps back and figure out what really *is* right," the pressure is going to mount but the product will indeed be better for it.

Try to imagine something at Apple so far down the line in importance that no way would Steve Jobs concern himself with it.

Now try this on for size:

There is a young man in Los Angeles by the name of Ian Maddox who works on the *Warehouse 13* television show on the Syfy channel. Before that he was a sales rep and "key holder" (aka assistant manager) at the Apple store in Pasadena. Shortly after he started there, a work crew began showing up every night after the last customer had left. They tore up the flooring section by section and laid new tile—dark gray granite imported from Italy, personally selected by Steve himself, "very fancy for a retail store," Ian says. A couple of days after the job was finished, early in the morning before the store opened, the managers were walking around in a state of high alert. Even the regional manager showed up.

And there he was: Steve Jobs himself, come to inspect the tiles, with four or five people trailing him.

Steve was not pleased. The tiling had looked fine when it was first laid but as soon as customers started walking across it, large, ugly splotches had begun to appear. Instead of making the place look classy, the tile created a dumpy, uncared-for look.

The employees were cowering, trying to take in the scene and watch Steve's reaction while pretending to be busy. He wasn't just dissatisfied, he was furious, fuming, ordering it be done over.

The next night, the work crew was back, tearing up the flooring and starting a complete redo. This time they used a different sealant and ordered a different product to be used for cleaning the tile.

When I heard this story, I smiled; I couldn't imagine any other CEO of a global company who would take the trouble to inspect the flooring in a company store, yet it seemed so typical of Steve, the master of details.

I think of that episode now and then, and ask myself, "Have I said recently, 'It's not what I asked for, but I guess it will be good enough'?" It's a way of checking myself on whether I'm being as demanding about the details, as demanding about perfection, as my model, Steve Jobs.

Ian also had another Steve Jobs story, one that reflects a different side of Steve's business personality. While working at the Apple store, Ian received an e-mail one day that surprised him. A customer he had helped had been pleased, and impressed enough to shoot an e-mail to Steve Jobs praising the service. The e-mail Ian received was from Steve, cc'd to the customer. The entire message read:

great job

Just that. No capital letter, no period, no signature. Ian says, "It was enough."

Again, how many CEOs of large companies do you think take the time to give a pat on the back to someone that far down the line?

Learning from Mistakes

As the Mac team grew closer to a machine with hardware that worked and software that performed all the needed functions and didn't crash, Steve came in one day for a demo, and he wasn't happy.

"What's that noise?" he asked.

Nobody knew what he was talking about. There wasn't any noise, except for a quiet hum from the fan.

Steve wasn't having any of it. Every other personal computer had a noisy fan. The Macintosh was going to be completely silent.

The engineers tried to explain to him: The Mac couldn't run without a fan. It would overheat and burn out.

Steve insisted: No fan.

Engineers started showing up in my office telling me I had to talk to Steve, I had to change his mind. Every engineer on the team insisted the Mac had to have a fan. The whole organization disagreed with him but he wouldn't change.

The engineers went back to their lab benches and started redesigning the Mac to run without a fan. The planned launch date came and went. The Macintosh would finally be introduced to the world five months late.

Steve had been right in principle. A completely quiet computer is a joy to use, but the penalty was too great. Again Steve would learn a valuable lesson. Details matter, it's worth waiting to get it right, but there are times when you have to weigh the benefit of getting it right against the cost of being late to market. Steve would continue to delay products to get them right, but he would publicly acknowledge that he would never again put himself in the position of allowing so great a delay.

To some Macintosh critics and even some of the company's avid boosters, those early Macs with their inevitable overheating problems were dubbed "beige toasters."

But all of the major products that would come later, from the iPod on, incorporate lessons Steve learned from building those first Macs— lessons about the process of getting products into the hands of the consumer, pricing, and others, were all based on experiences from those product-creator-in-training days.

Those were not Steve's only major gaffes on the Mac. He decided that in addition to creating the hardware and the software, he also wanted to *build* the computers. The factory would cost $20 million; the Apple board was reluctant, since nobody really believed the Macintosh would see the light of day—but the decision to approve was made a little easier since Apple had $200 million in the bank thanks to the stellar sales of the Apple II.

Steve found an existing factory building in nearby Fremont, little more than a half-hour drive from Cupertino, and set about having it redesigned as a fully automated plant to assemble the Macintosh. (Though the technology history books always refer to it as a factory, in fact it was really an assembly plant—the components were actually manufactured in Japan and elsewhere, and shipped to Fremont.)

He personally worked with the engineers designing the various automated machines, as usual becoming involved in detailed decisions about the functions each machine would perform and how they would be controlled. He was like a kid waiting for Christmas morning when a new machine arrived and was being installed. He could hardly wait to get to Fremont and see it in operation. His huge fascination with robotics seemed to grow out of that fascination he found in the human hand. In the final weeks before the plant went into production, he and I drove over there together about three times a week.

But this part of the story doesn't have a happy ending. If Steve had stopped early on and applied his very keen analytical powers, he would have recognized that Macintosh sales would have had to be astronomic for the plant to make financial sense. I think it probably cost about $20,000 to build each Mac that came out of the plant. The Macs were selling for about $2,000 each; do the arithmetic. It was a tremendously costly decision and would contribute to a massive problem when the Macintosh early on did not sell well.

But give Steve credit: It was another mistake he would never make again.

Small Change, Big Result

I appreciated Steve's insightfulness all the more because I had been exposed to examples earlier in my career. During my Intel days, I was in an executive meeting with the three founders of the company—Andy

Grove, Gordon Moore, and Bob Noyce (who was one of the inventors of the semiconductor).

Andy held up a competitor's semiconductor chip and said, "Look at this—it looks much better than our product. Our semiconductors have much better technology but this has a better case, better lettering, and all the contacts are gold. They're killing us with a product that isn't as good but *looks* better."

The semiconductor is a product that lives inside a computer or other electronic device. Even though the user never sees it, everyone in the meeting understood Intel needed to do something. They put a major plan in place to make the product appearance appropriate to the quality of the technology. Then they launched a major awareness campaign: the "Intel Inside" program.

Intel had been number four in the semiconductor market. With these efforts, they became number one.

It's no exaggeration to say that Steve Jobs has become so effective as a corporate leader and has created such a stream of extraordinary products because he is so focused on paying attention to even the smallest details and getting every detail right.

To Steve, *everything* matters. He will keep innovating to get closer and closer to his ideal, his vision of perfection, which almost always goes beyond what everyone else considers the currently achievable reality.

The process is time-consuming, it's maddening to the product creators who work for him, but it is an absolutely essential element of his success.

PART II

TALENT RULES

Teaming

"Pirates! Not the Navy"

I should have known it would hardly be your typical business product retreat. The oversized glass windows in the second-floor restaurant of the Carmel Inn gave everyone in the room a perfect view of the sparkling blue swimming pool. A bunch of young guys and a couple of young women were happily cavorting in the water below—stark naked. At eight in the morning, no less. Most of the diners didn't know where to look. Two dignified, gray-haired old ladies lingering over their coffee appeared to be in shock. I was almost as surprised as they were. Those kids out there splashing and hooting were members of the Macintosh team.

Forming a Team Culture

Every leader and every manager wants his or her people to work together, all pulling in the same direction, supporting each other, everybody pitching

in to do their part in achieving the goal of the group. Yes, the business
of the swimming pool was way over the top, not exactly the best example of what a leader should be striving for . . . but it certainly did
show that Steve had indeed created a sense of community among the
Macintosh group.

By this time, the Mac team had grown from the original core group of
five people formed to create a breakaway computer, to about thirty, including the newbies Steve had been adding to the teams. He had planned
this offsite to make sure everybody was on the same wavelength and
moving in the same direction.

 These folks, mostly twenty-somethings, were being challenged to
come up with completely fresh, original ideas in what could be called
a near-hostile setting: within the confines of a company thriving on a
product line that Steve now saw as dated and no longer relevant. The
skinny-dipping should have come as no surprise. He had scoured the halls
of Apple and elsewhere for people with the courage to be different, to
be unconventional, to go beyond. I saw the naked swimming as a sign
he was succeeding.

Elements of Team Building

As everyone walked into the opening session of the business retreat in
Carmel, guys and gals were standing by with handouts: Each arriving
team member was handed a T-shirt imprinted with what was to become
the iconic logo of the Mac team:

 Pirates! Not the Navy

I never did ask Steve where that line came from. I now think it may have
been a line made up by the late Jay Chiat, the incredibly talented co-

founder of Chiat/Day, the ad agency that through the years was to work such magic for Steve and Apple. But it was Steve who took it up as a catchphrase that would stir the troops. He recognized it as a rallying cry that would help build a cohesive team, a team of people who would bond and rely on one another.

And he succeeded. For Steve, product retreats were an amazing opportunity for bringing together people working on various aspects of the project who would not normally meet. These offsites fostered a sense of belonging and "We're all in this together" throughout the organization. Over three days, the team bonded by spending every waking minute together—eating, playing, and brainstorming.

Steve made a heartfelt speech celebrating their unique talents and appealing to their sense of playing a key role in building something revolutionary.

The "Pirates" T-shirt was just one of hundreds I would see during my tenure at the company. Apple would become known as a company that celebrated just about everything—product milestones, meeting goals, sales growth, new product introductions, new key people. And handing out T-shirts or sweatshirts to commemorate some milestone or achievement became a trademark of Apple. I think I must have collected a hundred of them myself over the years. And there's actually a coffee-table book filled with nothing but photographs of Apple T-shirts.

The Virtue of Small, Product-Focused Teams

Steve instinctively understood that some projects need the heat and intensity generated by bringing together a small number of talented people and allowing them to work free of the usual restrictions. In the right circumstances, driven by the right kind of courage, pirates can achieve what "the Navy" just can't do. He expected all team members to unleash their full creative and artistic talents. (Later he'd use this approach for the teams on *all* projects.)

His plan from early on was that the Mac group would never grow larger than a hundred people. "If we need to hire somebody with a particular expertise, somebody else will have to go," he said. He knew the danger of a work group growing so large that it would begin to erupt with organizational road bumps that would slow everything down. But the explanation he preferred to give was that "It's hard to know the names of more than a hundred people." One more minimalist attitude from his Buddhist beliefs. But of course, he was right. A large organization falls into the traps of duplication, too many layers of approval, and barriers that get in the way of communication and a free flow of ideas. Steve saw that already happening in the rest of Apple. He didn't want any of it. In fact, even then he said that what he wanted was to prove the "start-up" small-team concept with the success of the Macintosh, and then use that leverage to spread this product-oriented, small-team thinking to the rest of Apple.

"Pirates" wasn't just about the product—it captured the outlaw free-thinking revolutionary spirit Steve wanted to harness. He would talk about the future of Apple, worried that as it grew, it would become just another vanilla company.

His high expectations applied to everyone, from engineering to sales to accounting to production. Just as it took the ingenuity of hundreds and hundreds of visionary minds to put three men on the moon, Steve depended on every Macintosh employee for their own valuable spin and contribution to reach his ultimate goal.

That was the culture of a product-focused team. It would be essential, he said, if Apple was going to continue as a place of vibrant ideas, inspiring products, and at the same time a great place to work.

A large part of the Mac group's extraordinary camaraderie was also the result of Steve walling his people off from interference from the rest of the company. As a self-contained unit, the Mac team had its own designers, programmers, engineers, production staff, documentation writers, and advertising and promotion specialists. The upside of being part of a small product group, particularly when you may be working sixteen-hour days, is to have a comfortably close relationship with the

others in the group. This builds accountability. It becomes more personal, and keeps every individual absolutely determined to keep up with
the rest of the team.

Steve dreamed of the time that Apple could slash its way through
to a much simpler management structure, with fewer approval levels,
fewer people needing to sign off on every decision.

He used to tell me, "Apple should be the kind of place where anybody can walk in and share his ideas with the CEO." That pretty much
summed up his management style. But he knew he didn't have all the
answers. I can't even guess at how many hours he and I spent together
talking about how to keep people working as if it were their own company, their own product.

The Art of Bonding:
Advancing with Retreats

At the conclusion of the Carmel retreat, all the participants left with
two water glasses etched with the Apple logo. Those who had newly
joined Apple or the Macintosh group—like me—left our first retreat
completely fired up, feeling like a full-fledged team member. Everyone
seemed extremely positive. I had been to lots of corporate gatherings
but had never seen anything that came even close to this experience.
Not only had it clearly moved the Macintosh ahead, but it had achieved
the goal of creating feelings of camaraderie, respect, and a "we're-in-
this-together" sense of mutual support.

As I had seen at the retreat, Steve was a master at turning the cliché
of "team building" into an art form. He took a standard business-
as-usual ritual and reinvented it—just as he did for the products he made
and the motivation of the teams he led. He approached a business meeting as a total experience—as one more essential element in creating
the product.

Steve loved product retreats. He built them into the actual work schedule, hosting them about every three months for the entire growing Mac team. There was plenty of play time and relaxing built into retreat schedules, but the business sessions followed a pretty strict schedule. Every member was expected to be present. Debi Coleman, the Stanford MBA who kept track of Mac's budgets, was also keeper of the agenda at retreats and in charge of making sure the sessions moved along in an orderly way.

One by one, each team leader—for hardware, software, marketing, sales, finance, PR—would present a brief status report and timeline, explaining where they were in terms of schedule. If their team was falling behind, they went through whatever delays or problems they were encountering, and offered some ideas for how they thought they could get back on track. Everybody was free to chip in with suggestions. The idea was to air any problems openly and get the whole group thinking about how to solve them. It was all about the Mac, not about anybody's title or position.

The Leader as Pirate-in-Chief

Steve was the ringmaster of this circus, and he cracked a ringmaster's whip. He was always looking for something specific from each group to match the quality he wanted. He brought out the creative genius in so many people and led them to work in harmony. He was surrounding himself with people who fit into his style and philosophy, and who were willing (most of the time, at least) to let him lead the parade.

Yet at the same time, he encouraged open discussion. There was plenty of rancorous debate but plenty of laughter, too. The only times I saw Steve get really frustrated was when he felt someone wasn't being direct or forthright. Discussions might get heated, but—despite what you might read elsewhere—the overall tone of the meetings was always civil . . . though Steve was never reluctant about being sharp with some-one who offered a suggestion he thought was off base. He had such deep knowledge and insight into every aspect of the Macintosh that very little got by him. And he never was very patient with anything he considered stupid or ill-informed.

As I had seen in my former jobs at traditional companies, most busi-ness meetings tend to be run along lines dictated by the organizational structure. If the boss says the cow is purple, most of the time no one is going to point out that he has seen the animal, it's not actually a cow, and it's orange. Steve didn't buy that; if you had an idea, you spoke up. It didn't matter to him from which lowly staffer the idea, criticism, or suggestion was coming from as long as it was sensible and informed. One engineer remembers that "Steve often would initiate a meeting or discussion in a provocative, intense manner, but become more conver-sational once he determined you were not a bozo. I saw him do this in company-wide meetings where, in a drill-sergeant-like manner, he would find something to harp on at the beginning of the meeting to set the tone, and then shift into an inspirational posture."

Years later, one-time Apple executive Jean-Louis Gassé endorsed Steve's management style with a memorable phrase: "Democracies don't make great products—you need a competent tyrant." People who worked for Steve forgave him, or at least tolerated his style, in part be-cause more than anything else, he was a *product* tyrant, totally dedicated to delivering the products he envisioned.

Even pirates need a captain. And it helped that the grand poo-bah, the big boss, chairman of the company, wasn't "Mr. Jobs" but just plain "Steve." He gave the orders but made everyone feel that "he's one of us." He dropped in way too frequently to ask those painful and some-times embarrassingly detailed questions. Yes, at times the engineers in particular felt a little like they were in kindergarten.

What mattered, though, was that he wasn't sitting in an office issuing orders, he was right there—in the coalmine, so to speak, working right alongside everyone else. Every visit, every question, made the intense level of his concern and involvement perfectly clear. He cared deeply about every aspect of making the Mac a great product in every way down to the smallest detail. His actions proved that every single day. Even when he wasn't satisfied, it was always clear he was acting from a conviction that *everything is important*—that success is in the details.

Of course, one of his measures of dedication, especially for the hacker-engineers of the Mac team, was how many hours a day you were willing to put in. Sixteen hours? Fine. All weekend? Why not? (A harshly demanding but creatively successful Disney executive Steve would later work with supposedly told people, "If you don't come to work on Saturday, don't bother coming on Sunday." In other words, don't bother coming back, ever.)

If you truly believed you were changing the course of the industry and maybe the course of history, you'd work ridiculous hours, practically give up any other life for the duration, and consider yourself among the chosen, the privileged.

As we were walking away from one of his drop-ins on members of the engineering team, Steve looked at me and said, "I know they complain about me but they're going to look back on this as the best time of their lives. They just don't know it yet. But I do. This is a blast."

I said, "Steve, don't kid yourself. They know it and love it!"

Learning to Acknowledge a Bad Decision and Move Ahead

But even Steve wasn't infallible in assessing people. One near-disastrous decision for the Macintosh came from pursuing a path in part because he admired and respected the central figure of the episode.

The Macintosh would need a hard drive. Steve kept pretty much up to date on what computer components were available, and what was new and hot. But the pickings among hard drives, as far as he was concerned, were pretty slim. He didn't see anything he liked, nothing good enough to be selected as a crucial part of the Macintosh.

Then one day he introduced me to a visitor, a German man he had obviously taken a liking to, a very sharp guy who was or had been with Hewlett-Packard, and who had a strong background in hard drives. (My apologies to the gentleman: I no longer remember his name.)

Steve has always liked product-oriented people. Even more important is his being sure that you buy into his vision. That's major, something he has to be certain about with every key player. If he's confident about that, it's okay if you disagree with him, so long as you are in tune with his vision and direction.

Out of his sense of confidence in the hard-disk man, Steve fell victim to what someone later called "a serious case of the 'Not Invented Here' syndrome." He hired the man to design a new, state-of-the-art hard drive that would then be manufactured for the Mac at some nearby location in Silicon Valley.

One of my positions at IBM had been as a senior manager at their largest hard-drive plant, in San Jose, California. It's a business no outsider should try to get into. You have to worry about substrates and mechanical arms and precision. They are devilishly hard products to design and manufacture. As just one item, the read-heads ride about a hair's width from the spinning disk; the tolerances in manufacture can be a nightmare. It's a very difficult task to build drives that work properly.

I said to Steve, "I really believe we should not be in the hard-drive business. I believe we should find one." And the head of Mac hardware, Bob Bellville, was pressuring him about the same thing. But Steve was determined. Somebody came up with the code name "Twiggy," and the effort got underway, staffing up with what would become a workforce of some *three hundred* people.

I had a conversation with Belleville. We were on the same wavelength and he thought he might have an answer. Sony had a new 3.5-

inch hard drive that they had developed for Hewlett-Packard and were already shipping. One of Belleville's engineers, who had come from HP, might be able to ask his contacts there to loan one of the drives for us to test.

Bob soon had the drive in hand. He was pleased, saying it could be made to work in the Mac. While his engineers went to work on an interface, negotiations got underway with Sony; the company was only too pleased at the idea of doing a project for Apple.

Work on Twiggy and the Sony drive went ahead in parallel—with no one telling Steve, of course, about the Sony project. Bob made quick trips to Japan now and then as needed, and one of the Sony engineers came to Cupertino on occasion to discuss technical specifications. That all went well until one day when the Sony engineer was in Bob's office. As they talked, Bob heard a familiar voice in the hall, approaching his office.

He jumped up, pulled open the door of a janitor's closet, and frantically gestured for the engineer to step in. The poor guy was completely bewildered. Why, in the middle of a meeting, should he allow himself to be shut up in a closet!?

But he trusted Bob. He stepped in. Bob shut the door on him, sat back down and pretended to be hard at work as Steve walked in. The engineer stayed quietly in the dark closet until Steve left.

I laugh about that scene every time I think of it.

Months later, I showed up for a Twiggy product review in the conference room of the Mac building. Steve's hard drive guy went through the results of the testing. He was honest about it: The results were horrible. Twiggy was obviously a disaster.

Steve called a meeting with all the Mac team leaders, on the engineering side and the business side. When everybody was ganging up on him to cancel Twiggy, he turned to me and said, "Jay, I wish you could hover above the meeting and tell me what to do."

I said, "Fine. Let's take a walk outside."

We went for one of our walks—this one rather more sensitive than most. He trusted me to be candid, and I was. "Steve," I said, "you ought to kill the project. It's a ridiculous waste of money. And I will commit to place every one of the Twiggy people in other jobs."

We walked back into the meeting. Steve sat down and said, "Okay, Jay has decided to kill the project." I squirmed at his putting this on me but did my best not to show any reaction. He went on, "And he has committed to place all the people. Nobody will lose their job."

That was the end of Twiggy for the Macintosh. It was closed down. As I had promised, I leaned on my HR people and we found new jobs in other parts of Apple for all of the Twiggy group.

The Macintosh went to market with the Sony drive, which was probably half as expensive as the Twiggy would have been, and without the manufacturing overhead.

Ever since the Twiggy fiasco, Steve has been much more ready to buy from an outside supplier when the circumstances justify it. These days, to get a product to market more quickly, he'll often accept components or software from outside, and then move development inside Apple for later versions.

Twiggy taught him a lesson he has never forgotten.

There is a postscript to the Twiggy story. The Apple group developing the Lisa computer revived Twiggy, and used two of the Twiggy floppy drives in the original version of their computer. But the design problems that plagued the drives when they were supposed to go into the Mac had never been solved. Users found the drives slow and, worse, unreliable. The natives grew so restless that Apple finally offered the 6,000 or so early purchasers a free upgrade to a remodeled Lisa that replaced the two Twiggys with a Sony drive of less capacity but greater reliability.

Steve had found it tough to make the decision of canceling Twiggy. But he was vindicated: It had clearly been the right choice.

The All-Around Manager

Steve's concern with details applied not just to technical and design issues, but as well to dollars-and-cents issues, and this was a source of frustration for him. Debi Coleman, as CFO for the Mac group, was continually redoing her projections on sales. But at the same time, Apple Finance was doing its own projections, and the numbers never matched. They were trading information back and forth, supposedly always starting from the same assumptions but always coming up with different answers. Debi, very entrepreneurial, was committed to making sure the projections were solid. But every time she and Steve would sit down with the corporate CFO, Joe Graziano, it would be the same story all over again—apparently because there are a variety of ways to account for different items. (Not that it matters, but Joe was a CFO who drove a red Ferrari. I always thought that sent the wrong message!)

Steve never ceased to amaze me in these sessions: He always seemed to have a better handle on projections than the CFOs. And his demand for perfection of the data was just as strong as his demand for product perfection. He insisted that every aspect be as good as the product itself.

The Space Sets the Stage for the People

To a Steve Jobs, a team is more than the sum of its people. It's also affected by the work environment. The workspace itself can have a strong influence on how well the team functions. It isn't just a set of cubicles or work benches; the physical setting is part of creating the aura, the atmosphere of being special.

In 1981, the Mac group moved into a building on Bandley Drive that had previously been used by part of the Apple II group. The centerpiece of the new building was a large atrium. Steve put his office near the front entrance, with everyone else spread out in cubicles and labs formed in expanding arcs around him, placing Steve at the focal point like the conductor of an orchestra with his players arrayed before him. The atrium had a piano, video games, and a huge fridge stocked with bottles of fruit juice. It quickly became a place for the employees to meet and hang out. On display in the atrium was Steve's old original BMW motorcycle, still in mint condition—a symbol of great design and functionality but also, as far as I was concerned, a symbol that this particular team had a very different kind of leader. Pixar and Google would later receive lots of press coverage by creating similar kinds of environments for their employees; Steve was, as with so many other things, out in front.

On the other hand, though this doesn't sound like something you'd expect of a Buddhist, before his team moved in, Steve actually told me he wanted to bring in an exorcist to get rid of the demons in the structure; he was absolutely serious about this idea. It was as if he thought that the Apple II group was somehow tainted and had left behind bad vibes.

I thought if anyone found out, it would open us up to ridicule—one more thorn in the side of the rest of Apple. Fortunately he was willing to listen to reason and gave up the idea. (I'd say maybe he just made the suggestion as a way of teasing me, except that when it came to business, and anything about the Macintosh in particular, Steve rarely showed a sense of humor.)

Corporate Culture, Old Style

Looking back, I don't think the youngsters on the team realized how unconventional the culture was that Steve had created for the Mac group.

For me, it was a delight and something of a small miracle, because I was forever noticing how different the "Pirates" attitude was from the companies where I had previously worked.

When I was at IBM, even with all the incredibly smart people at that company—as I've said, I was surrounded by many brilliant minds for years—most of us were so far removed from the actual product that we tended to lose sight of just exactly what we were working toward. IBM was the fourth or fifth largest corporation in the world and had 400,000 employees. Most of them I assume were comfortable with the IBM culture; I never felt as if I quite fit in, even after going through their executive training program. I never got caught up in the typical business-executive kind of concerns.

Over one long holiday, I grew a beard and didn't shave it off when I returned. My superiors weren't quite sure what to make of me—this guy in the standard IBM uniform of suit, white shirt, and tie, whose new beard was a slap in the face. My IBM colleagues used to say, "We have wild ducks . . . but they fly in formation."

I eventually became very frustrated about their lack of interest in new product areas. Sitting around a conference table in a high-level meeting one day, Chairman of the Board Frank Carey listened to a suggestion of mine and told me, "IBM is like a supertanker, very large and hard to maneuver. When you set a course, you can't change easily. It takes twenty-one miles to turn, and sixteen miles to stop."

When I heard that, I knew I didn't belong there.

At Apple, I never felt like just a policy guy. Absolutely I was interested in the business side of the equation, and could make solid plans and translate them to work in a smoothly operating company, but I also immediately recognized the significance of the new direction in computing the team was driving toward. The phenomenon of Steve's focus and passion for every single element of the product was something I had never seen before. And I wholeheartedly bought into it.

If You Became Very Rich, Would You Still Manage the Same Way?

I'd be willing to bet that most people who win a big bundle in the lottery immediately tell their boss that they are quitting, and never go back to work. What would you do if you suddenly became very rich?

Two weeks before Christmas in 1980, Steve Jobs received a huge present, and so did quite a few other people at the company. When Apple Computer shares were offered on the stock exchange, the public clamored to buy with the same fervor that the iPod and iPhone would later unleash. The first hour saw the sale of 4.6 million shares; by the end of the first day, it was being heralded as the most successful public stock offering in history, and the most oversubscribed IPO since the Ford Motor Company had gone public nearly thirty years earlier.

In a single day, Steve had become one of the world's richest self-made men. He liked to tell people, "I was worth a million dollars when I was twenty-three, ten million when I was twenty-four, and over two hundred million when I was twenty-five."

The previous year, Xerox had invested in Apple. (It was a condition of the deal that Steve and the engineers were allowed to make those industry-changing visits to Xerox PARC.) I hope the two people at Xerox who were responsible for making that investment decision were suitably rewarded: the Xerox stake of $1 million was suddenly worth in the neighborhood of $30 million.

The striking thing is that Steve's sudden riches didn't seem to change him in any significant way. The now–mega millionaire cofounder and board chairman of a Fortune 500 company still came to work in his traditional T-shirt, Levis, and Birkenstocks.

Okay, he'd put on a suit now and then for a meeting with a banker or someone he wanted to impress. But he hardly ever talked about money or possessions. He already had a house, a Mercedes coupe, and a BMW motorcycle with orange pom-poms on the handlebars that he had bought when the company received venture capital investments a year earlier. By his own measures, he had the few acquisitions he had any interest in.

When he traveled, he flew first class. But that was standard Apple policy: In those days, *every* employee flew first class—not just executives and managers but engineers and "area associates" (which is what Apple called the secretaries). The company was so flush with money that there was no health plan; when you had a medical expense, whether for a doctor's visit or a serious operation, you just submitted the bills and Apple covered the costs.

To Steve, work wasn't about making enough money to retire. It wasn't about making money, period. It was about leading his pirate team to create a great product. Through the years he would become richer and richer, yet clearly never lose the dedication to creating awesome products.

On Being a Pirate

Looking back, I admit that I'm flattered Steve was so determined to bring me into Apple and even more into the Macintosh group. I was always a pirate, but didn't know it until Steve came up with the term. I had been labeled a "wild duck" at IBM because of what must have seemed like my sometimes-out-of-step opinions about the business, products, and leadership. I also hated politics and bureaucracy and always drove my staff at Apple to keep bureaucratic thinking out of everything they did. At the same time, I was driven by the kind of incredible passion that marked the rest of the Macintosh team.

It didn't take me long to realize that Steve was following the principle of seeking out the very best talent and signing them up if he possibly could. That he saw me as meeting that standard, just at a time when I was available, was one of the very best things that has happened to me.

My experience at Apple convinced me that no matter what businesses I might be in later, I would always try to give everyone working for me something like the experience of being a pirate at a start-up. Pirates accept a demand for high standards from their leader. They accept a demand for perfection, and they strive to achieve it.

Tapping
Talent

If you were starting a new school, you would want to hire the very best teachers you could get. If you were starting a website aimed at people who compete in horse shows, you'd hope to staff up with fine riders who were or had been medal-class winners and had won Best of Show trophies. And so on.

That's easy to say but obviously not so easy to do. Yet it's one of the keys to the success of Steve Jobs. Each time he has been faced with the challenge, he has managed to come up with extraordinary people. A few examples will reveal the principles that have made him so successful at this.

The list of principles obviously begins with evaluating the person's past achievements—looking for evidence of a proven talent in some area or skill that the company or a particular project has a need for. That's a given. Everybody who has ever written a résumé, read a résumé, or hired at least one employee already understands this one. At Apple in those days, the résumé was not as important as you might expect.

Seeking People Who
Are Excited About the Project

For me, one of the funniest hiring stories of Steve's career—and it really sums up his approach—is about one of his early hires on the Mac team. One day software engineer Andy Hertzfeld got a call from Scotty—Mike Scott, Apple's president—to come in and see him. That scared Andy: Only a few days before, Scotty had decided that the company wasn't meeting goals and needed to cut expenses, so he had just fired half of Apple's engineers; the occasion came to be known in Apple mythology as "Black Wednesday."

The remaining engineers, Andy included, were both unhappy and afraid for their own jobs. But when Andy showed up for the appointment, Scotty made it clear that he didn't want Andy to leave and asked what it would take to convince him to stay. Andy said he'd like to be part of the Mac team. Two of his best buddies, Burrell Smith and Brian Howard, had recently joined the Mac unit. Andy was told he'd have to meet with Steve first.

Steve didn't waste any time. As Andy described it to me later, Steve began with, "Are you any good? We only want really good people working on the Mac and I'm not sure you're good enough. . . . I hear you're creative. Are you really creative?"

Rather than taking offense, Andy stood up to his interrogator on that score and made it clear as well that he was very much behind the Mac project. Steve told Andy he'd get back to him.

Only a couple of hours later, Steve showed up at Andy's workstation and congratulated him. Andy was now officially part of the Mac team, effective immediately. Andy said it would take him a couple of days to finish up what he was working on.

Steve wasn't going to wait. He literally pulled the plug on Andy's computer, picked up the machine, took it out of the building, and tossed it into the back of his silver Mercedes, with a bewildered Andy following in his wake. As Steve drove Andy to Mac headquarters, "Texaco Towers," at the corner of Stevens Creek and the Saratoga-Sunnyvale Road, he made it clear the Macintosh was going to be the best thing ever to hit the computer industry.

Andy had impressed Steve with his directness and his fascination with the product. Recommendations from Burrell and Brian of the Mac engineering team, whom Steve had questioned about Andy before making the hire, were also crucial.

Steve doesn't hesitate or waste time once he's made up his mind about somebody. And he was right. Andy turned out to be as important a member of the Mac development team as anyone.

Although he operates from the gut level when hiring, he's also very thorough. Before an interview with attorney Nancy Heinen—who later became the company's general counsel—Steve asked to see some contracts she had written so he could evaluate the "aesthetics" of her work.

Sometimes after an interview by Steve, I'd talk to the candidate myself. Most of the people I talked with didn't even feel the time with Steve had been an interview; in their eyes, it was more like a college lecture or a VC pitch on Apple products, followed by a final exam of you explaining how you were going to contribute to Mac and the team.

High IQs Only, Please

Beyond hiring for capabilities, Steve makes sure his hires are true Apple enthusiasts capable of thriving in an intense start-up environment. It's become easier to find the right talent today because so many potential candidates have information posted on the web. Of course we didn't have that luxury in the early days of the Mac.

On the other hand, Steve was, from when I first knew him, only willing to have around him people who, in his judgment, had "a three-digit

IQ" and were not—his terminology again—"bozos." He was intensely uncomfortable with people he thought didn't measure up. Unfortunately, he could be entirely tactless about this. If he considered you to be bright, capable, and making a contribution, you could tell him what you thought or that there was a better way than what he was telling you to do, and he would listen. But if he decided you were a bozo, you'd better block your ears and get away fast.

He had only those two categories, though: If you weren't brilliant, you were that other thing, a bozo. But with Steve, no matter how brilliant he knew you were, one remark that didn't, by his standard, measure up, and he'd immediately label you a bozo. Even in front of other people. Of course, by the next day, or even the same afternoon, he would have forgotten and things would be on an even keel again. It always hurt but people learned to take it in stride.

By now Steve figures he has probably hired several thousand people in the course of his career. But recruiting is still tough. Interviews are too short to give you as much information as you really need about candidates. For Steve, often the actual responses to interview questions are less important than *how* the person responds. Above all, he needs to be convinced that the candidate has really gone head-over-heels for Apple.

But Steve wasn't the only person who hired people. We had to ask ourselves how we could extend solid ideas about hiring and working together from one successful workgroup to the entire organization. We worked really hard to identify and create a paper on "Apple Values," which is what we called the document spelling out Apple's corporate culture. When it was finished, I had it sent to Apple facilities, and to all new facilities as the company expanded all over the world. I spent a lot of time overseas, especially in Europe, making sure the company's international hiring standards were as rigorous as they were in the

United States. I would personally visit all the facilities everywhere to make sure that the same style, and value set, were in place worldwide. I also made sure all our recruiters were in tune with the standards set in Cupertino.

A Different Kind of Hiring

Because he was trying to invent a new usage model for personal computing, Steve was constantly looking for additional people with specialized skills. He knew that he needed a class-act technologist and charged me with finding someone. I asked around; a headhunter sent me the résumé of Bob Belleville, who was head of technology for office printers at PARC. The man was incredibly intelligent about computer systems. Though he was a thirty-something, he looked more like thirteen. When I sent him in to meet with the boss, Steve told him, "I hear you're great, but everything you've done so far is crap. Come work for me." Despite that put-down, he did.

The hackers of the original Mac team were geniuses but they didn't have the big picture; Belleville had it. He often found himself confronted by some very difficult situation with the hackers on one side and Steve on the other. He had a quietly effective style for convincing people to do things his way. To convince Steve of something, he wouldn't just try to explain it in words. Instead, he'd use his technowizardry to whip together some mock-up or working electronic demo to show off his idea.

Bob was very effective in getting people to perform because of his quiet way of convincing. He was brilliant, but never used his intelligence for leverage—his goal was always to find a way to make the right outcome happen. And he usually succeeded.

I spent a lot of time with Bob; he often came to me for advice on how to convince Steve of something. But from the time he came onboard, he played a key role as facilitator between Steve and the hackers, in a

way paralleling my role as facilitator between the Mac team and everyone else.

For me, the hiring of Bob was an example of how important it is to
go beyond the traditional hiring information and find out what this person's underlying talents are, trying to understand what they could bring
to the organization.

Using Your Products as
a Casting Call for Talent

Steve's fiercely protective love of Apple products has turned the products
themselves into a casting call for some of the world's most talented and
creative people. Steve's ability to create iconic personal technology complements his ability to attract the talent who can realize his vision.

That didn't apply only to hiring engineers. To state what's now obvious but wasn't at the time, design talent was as important to Steve as
engineering talent. Team member Andy Hertzfeld had gone to high
school in Pennsylvania with a girl named Susan Kare, who had since
then become a graphic designer and Artist with a capital A. When the
Mac group recognized a need for someone creative to dream up the icons
for the Mac displays, Andy put her name in the hopper. Interviewing
her, Steve decided that Susan's talent, passion, and flair were more important than the fact that her background was light on technology. He
accepted her as a key part of the Mac team.

Almost twenty years later, Susan remembered Steve as "pushing back
and being critical . . . to see if you had explored every option" and that
"when he's happy and pleased with an idea, he can make you feel great."

One weekend Steve had dinner at a restaurant in San Francisco called
Ciao. He was captivated by the Picasso-like graphics on their menu.
Monday morning he arrived at work bursting to share his enthusiasm.

He sought out Susan Kare. Inspired by his suggestions and even more by his enthusiasm, she captured the essence and simplicity in everything from the readily understood icons (think of the trash-can icon), to the typeface, to the look and color of the case. The future of the Macintosh screen appearance was born the night Steve by chance went to eat at Ciao restaurant. And then it was as if Susan had opened a cornucopia of plenty and shown him the contents. With Susan's help, Steve experienced the joy of creating a product that could delight the eye and win worldwide admiration for its design. This was his high, his LSD.

If the distinctive Apple approach to design was born the night Steve happened to go have dinner at Ciao, it was Susan who unfolded the implications of this approach and really made it work. The joy of creating an eye-catching product that would win worldwide admiration for its design is one of the things he now lives for. Never again would he be satisfied with boxy designs like the Apple IIc or IIe, even though they were significantly better looking than the IBM PC. And he is still and forever on the lookout for other Susans, people whose talent and artistry infuse everything they do.

Every team needs the spark of at least a few truly creative people who "think different"—different enough to set an example for everyone else.

Talent Finds Talent

One of the greatest things about finding good people is that they become your best recruiters. They are the people most likely to know others who have the same values and sense of style that you and they themselves do. A good "Pirate" generally has a friend or relative who is just as good. Steve used to say to me that "great engineers are a huge multiplier."

Steve and I started a couple of programs to make sure we got the right talent to work on the Mac. We gave employees a five-hundred-dollar bonus if they recommended someone who got hired. We also used a "buddy system" that put each new recruit under the wing of someone else in the organization. We'd also send out the best employees we had hired in the past two years back to the schools they had graduated from to do recruiting.

Hiring "A" Players

When talking to a candidate for a job, Steve comes at things from unfamiliar angles, asking himself, "Does this person fit?" He's so wrapped up in the product that he carries a vision of who will be able to integrate themselves completely into the development team. He only wants to hire people whose work is able to stand up to his scrutiny and who don't feel threatened by pointed criticism actually aimed at making the end product not only better but the best.

He's unencumbered by predetermined opinions, biases, and processes. He meets candidates without a pre-set agenda. Sometimes I think this comes partly from what others with his Buddhist background call "beginner's mind"—the ability to see familiar things freshly. Also, during the Mac era, he was young, and therefore less likely to have a perspective that was already settled and locked-in. Somehow, he's been able to maintain that.

One of Steve's core principles is always to hire the best—"A-people," as he calls them. One of his mottoes was: "As soon as you hire a B, they start bringing in Bs and Cs." An A-person could be almost anyone with real talent. Steve hired Randy Wiggington, who wrote the code for MacWord, the first real Mac application, when he was still in high school. That didn't matter, because Randy was more than able to do the job.

• • •

Few people have been more important to Apple's success than a Brit named Jonathan Ive, though the story of Steve's "finding" him doesn't exactly fit the pattern of the other tales of talent scouting in these pages.

As a student in England, Jonathan ended up winning the student's award for design from the Royal Society of Arts. *Twice.* With the first one came a brief internship in the U.S. He found time to hop a flight to California and make the rounds of hot young design firms in Silicon Valley. After graduation, Ive joined a firm where he spent months working on the design for a bathroom sink (the details have been transformed along the way: accounts often describe it as a toilet). It's typical of him that he produced a great many different versions before finally settling on a design he was satisfied with.

Around the same time, a designer he had met on his earlier trip to Silicon Valley, Robert Brunner, had become chief of design at Apple. He had tried to hire Jony twice before; this time, Jony was on a low from the downer of working with people who found no pleasure from his innovative designs. He accepted Brunner's offer.

This was in the hiatus years. When Steve Jobs returned and began slashing projects, products, and people, Jony's head was on the line. Despite having designed the Newton, he had become Apple's design chief the year before. And Steve hated the look of most Apple products. He went on a headhunting expedition to find a new head of design.

Happily, before he had found what he was looking for, he began to recognize that he had a world-class designer already on salary. Instead of replacing Jonathan, Steve embraced him, confirmed him as chief designer of Apple's new age, and gave him the encouragement, the resources, and the support that have been a crucial factor in the success of Apple and its products ever since.

Today, Jony works in his locked-door design lab on the Apple campus, an area of gleaming aluminum and state-of-the-art design tools, manned by a small staff of some dozen lucky (or rather, uniquely talented) designers from half a dozen countries. He presides over the creation of one product after another that continue to achieve a dazzling brilliance of handsome looks executed in support of functionality. Jonathan Ive and his team continue to set a standard that no other company comes close to matching.

The remarkable point of the story is that Steve came so close to replacing him but recognized Ive's true talent in time.

Looking at what they've done since, it's obvious the people Steve found were not one-hit wonders. His hires went on to found other major technology firms. Jean Louis Gassée started Be, Mike Boisch started Radius, Guy Kawasaki started Garage.com . . . and those are just a few.

Donna Dubinsky had been a student at the Harvard Business School when in class one day she saw a demonstration of an Apple II computer running VisiCalc. She had worked in banking and knew how arduous it could be to do spreadsheets by hand: "What if the interest was 10 percent instead of 9.5?" Getting the answer to a simple question like that could require recalculating every number on the page. So she understood the potential: "Every banker will want this."

She had also worked on the financing side of the cable TV businesses, which "showed me the value of being in a growth area." Put those two elements together and, she says, "I knew this was it"—Apple was the company she wanted to work for. One small problem: Apple had never hired anyone from Harvard's B-School. She applied for an interview but "I was rejected. They just wanted technical people."

The day of the interviews, a determined Donna sat outside the interview room all day. "Every time the lady would step out," she says, "I'd try to speak to her." As Steve himself well knows, what's impossible can become possible if you're determined enough. "Finally, near the end of the day, she took pity on me and let me come in to talk to her." Despite the "technical people only" edict, Donna's perseverance had won the day.

Donna's enthusiasm for Apple and its products must have shown clearly. She was flown out for further interviews, and was offered a job on the business side, in Distribution Support, to start as soon as she had her MBA.

Reporting for work in Cupertino came with its surprises. She was used to the formal ways of the banking world. People above you in rank were addressed as "Mr." or "Ms." No files stacked on your desk. And, "You put on your suit coat just for going to the ladies room, in case you ran into a customer." At Apple, of course, she found the dress code was mostly shorts, T-shirts, and flip-flops.

In those days the company was expanding so fast that things tended to be chaotic. "By the time I got there," she says, "20 or 30 percent of the people were new, and the guy who hired me was already in a different job."

But Donna's background wasn't entirely conventional: In high school she had been in the marching band. She realized there is more than one way to run a business. This was a world of creativity. She found it "eye-opening."

"I was soon working dawn to dusk," she explains, "developing information systems and keeping product flowing."

Donna's contact with Steve was mostly in Forecast meetings. She vividly remembers a couple of his decisions that from her business background didn't make sense. She recalls that at one point, "We were moving from 300 dpi printers to 1200 or something—some generational shift. What to do with the old inventory? You cut the price and blow them away. You make money from customers who want the bargain."

Instead Steve said, "Take them off the list. People need to buy the new one."

Donna had discovered an important point about Steve. His choice violated basic Harvard-taught business principles but showed how he has always been all about what's good for the customer: "These printers are outdated, they're not what people should be buying, let's just get rid of them."

Through the years, Apple has proved to be a powerful training ground. Donna would become CEO of Palm, and cofounder of Handspring. *Fortune* nominated her to their "Innovators Hall of Fame."

She attributes her success in part to "the huge number of things" she learned from serving under Steve Jobs. "You've got to have great people. You've got to build great products. You need to create a management ethos of spontaneity and of celebrating successes."

But perhaps the most important lesson she learned is "how much difference a single person can make."

Courting Talent

Steve's full-blown ability to recognize and hire the best, most talented people has given rise to some other memorable tales.

In the early days of NeXT, Steve attempted to recruit video engineer Steve Mayer, who had worked with him when Steve was at Atari before he and Woz started Apple. Mayer agreed to go in and talk to Steve, and thought he seemed "devastated" that he was no longer at Apple but at the same time seemed "absolutely sure he was going to do something new and important."

Steve was courting rather than interviewing Mayer, a skill at which he is equally adept. He steered the conversation through what Mayer calls "the 'Imagine' process," with Steve spinning out a dramatic, highly visual storyline:

Imagine yourself reading a magazine, and it has an intriguing ad for a new computer.

Imagine that you make a call to the company to find out more about this new device. You're intrigued, and the company not only answers your questions but invites you to visit.

Imagine you pull into the driveway of the company, and approach the build-
ing to be greeted by a waiting receptionist.

You are escorted through the building, past the labs, and into the demo room
where the product is draped.

The product is revealed, and it is striking in appearance.

This high-tech *Arabian Nights* tale then morphed into a dialogue about the machine's most important features and uses.

But in fact, the product wasn't revealed to Mayer— because it didn't exist yet, and in any case, Steve wasn't going to show plans or models of what it might be like to anyone who wasn't yet on the payroll and under a confidentiality agreement.

To Mayer, this displayed a wonderful sense of theater that "takes you into the world of the product. He makes you share the vision of how the product will be used." It was typical: Steve always starts by envisioning the end product rather than working through the engineering details, which is how so many other high-tech products begin their lives.

Steve used a different tack with Apple senior manager Burt Cummings, who had said no when first contacted because he was in the process of being promoted to a director position, which at Apple was one step below vice president. Burt had developed and run the higher education program at Apple, and was told Steve wanted him to do the same for NeXT.

Burt says, "When I said no, the recruiter asked me if I'd come talk to Steve before making my final decision. I said sure."

When he went in for the meeting:

Steve and I chatted for a while and then he said that of course nobody was allowed to see the product until they signed on, but he could show me a piece of it.

I bit. He then said that the main unit was going to be separate from the keyboard and monitor, and that there was going to be a cable that connected it all up. This cable, he took pains to explain, contained the connections for the keyboard, mouse, video, audio, and power for the monitor. So five cables all combined into one.

He then brought out the actual cable, and it was slick. He held it in an inverted U and moved his hands up and down as though he was milking a cow, pointing out that it didn't kink at all.

He then told me I could run my hand over the cable while he "milked" it.

I did.

Burt says that as soon as he touched it, "I said I was in."

And then Burt adds, "This says a lot about how stupid I was"—meaning he thought afterward that Steve had snookered him—that he had been talked into taking the job by a bit of Stevian charm and hypnotism. (But I would always insist to people like Burt that they had not really gotten snookered; instead, "You just learned a lesson from the master product guy. It was the product that got you, not Steve."

Choosing People Who Are
Both Pirates and Team Players

In 1990, at a slightly later stage of his career, when Steve was searching for performance workstation engineers, he came across one young man with an impressive background. Jon Rubinstein, known as Ruby, after graduating from electrical engineering at Cornell University had entered the workplace with a job at Hewlett-Packard developing workstations. When Steve heard about him and tracked him down, Ruby was in charge of processor development of a graphics supercomputer. Running a team on a complex project suggests a leader who can take charge and get things done. When Steve identifies someone he thinks might turn into a key player, he doesn't leave recruiting in the hands of somebody from HR or an outside recruiting firm. He picks up the phone himself. Ruby said yes.

One of Ruby's professors at Cornell, Fred Schneider, didn't just teach Ruby but says he learned an important lesson from his one-time student—a lesson that offers an important clue about how Apple is able to design products so much better than anyone else. What Ruby taught him, the professor says, is that designing complex electronic systems is no different from designing a vacuum cleaner. "It has to be that easy to use. It has to be that easy, from the time you open the box." Schneider comments that "he and the folks at Apple have a very different model of doing business than any other computing company."

Ruby was to play a key role in the development of the iPod and subsequent products, as we'll see.

Creating an Atmosphere That Draws Talent

So what is it about Apple that attracts so many talented people? The pressure is intense and Steve's demands are at a constant fever pitch. But he is a genuine visionary, a for-real example of that overused term. If anyone in technology has established his credentials as an innovator, it's Steve.

It's the relentless emphasis on being the best that makes Apple so attractive to top people. They know they're going to be working on truly groundbreaking projects and doing more interesting things at Apple than elsewhere. The people Steve and Apple hire then become imbued with Steve's attitude that what's being done elsewhere isn't up to snuff. This feeling of superiority would be totally insufferable if the Apple team hadn't in fact been able to create many of the best consumer products anyone has ever seen.

Once Steve finds good people, he does everything he can to hold on to them. The tech business is as competitive as they come, and Steve has been criticized for apparently believing that all is fair in love and war. He's been accused of poaching key talent, such as iPod principal Jeff Robbin, from other companies. But he certainly doesn't intend to have the same thing happen to him. Indeed, for some time during the early iPod days, he refused to let journalists put Robbin's full name into print. That information was strictly off the record.

Acquiring Steve's Ways

Working with a person of Steve's drive and intensity, you soak up ideas and practices without being aware of it. Some years ago, after I had left Apple, I was looking to hire a product marketing manager for one of my start-ups. This person would be the liaison between sales and engineering, plus be our "senior customer rep." So he or she needed to have a technical background but also be able to talk on a sales level to the sales organization. One of my reps said he knew of a great guy whose company had just laid him off. So I set up an interview and was looking forward to meeting this man, touted to me as being very smart, with a master's degree from Stanford.

When he came in for an interview, what really impressed me was when the conversation got to a question about my company and the product. I discovered he knew almost as much about my product as I did. He had done thorough research, he had used the product, and he actually had some solid ideas on how to improve the user interface. I hired him and we in fact implemented some of his ideas.

In today's market, with all the Internet information about products and companies, it can be a wise move to hold out for a candidate who has taken the trouble to do the homework. In fact, if you were working at Apple, Steve Jobs would expect it of you.

• • •

I recently had a reminder that I started learning lessons on hiring from Steve back when I was first working with him. By chance I ran into a man named David Arella, who told me the story of how I had hired him for Apple. He had worked for the Environmental Protection Agency and then moved to the San Francisco city government while getting an MBA from Stanford. Looking for a new job, he sent out a lot of résumés and got a response from Apple, which surprised him because he didn't think he had much in the way of qualifications that would apply.

He says when he came in for the appointment with me, I studied his résumé, asked a few questions that didn't really sound like a job interview and then told him, "I think you could contribute here. I don't know what you would do—your background doesn't fit anything in particular for us." I quoted a salary to him, David says, and asked "Would you be willing to join us and we'll figure out where you could go?"

He started working on policy in the Compensation Department, eventually becoming head of HR for the Apple II group, with a multimillion-dollar budget. At our recent meeting, he said, "You didn't hire me because of my qualifications, you hired me despite them. It started me on a career path I'm still following." He then said, "I've probably told that story a hundred times."

To me, the story demonstrates that you didn't have to be around Steve for very long before his attitudes and practices started changing your way of working.

Sometimes there are people who appear to be all "Navy" but when you reach inside, you find a "Pirate" dying to be released. One such person was Grace Hopper. When I met Grace, she was in her sixties and a navy admiral, wearing her uniform proudly. She wasn't just navy in the "Navy versus Pirates" sense, she was the real thing. How much more navy can you get!?

Meeting her was a very special treat for me: She was one of my heroes. As part of the navy research center, she invented one of the very first computer programming languages, which became the basis of the very widely used COBAL, the software language that really revolutionized programming. When I met her, she was at first polite and nothing more. When I brought up the subject of software, she got this twinkle in her eye. I realized I was talking to a very bright and creative person whom I felt could very easily become a pirate.

It was a great reminder that in searching for talent, you mustn't be put off by first impressions but must probe to find the real person, sometimes discovering a pirate where you least expected.

Rewards for
the Pirates

Most corporations acknowledge employees by holding a little celebration for birthdays, employment anniversaries, and so on. But for a product-centric company like Apple, celebrations, rewards, and recognitions are focused around the company's stars: its talent and its products.

Steve truly cherishes his people. It's not just that he knows he couldn't be doing all these great things without them: He lets his people *know* he knows. The lengths Steve goes to shower recognition, appreciation, and reward on his people often left me in awe.

The most memorable example came when he told me, "Artists sign their work," and decided that the signatures of the original engineering team members would be etched on the inside of the cases of the first Macs. The signing party was held after a weekly staff meeting on February 10, 1982, with each person on the engineering team putting his or her signature on a big piece of drafting paper, including Steve Wozniak, using his familiar nickname, Woz.

FEBRUARY 10, 1982

Mac buyers would never see the signatures inside the case or even know they were there. But the engineers knew it, and that meant a lot to them. Even to this day, every time they see a classic Mac in someone's garage or in a computer museum, they have the satisfaction of knowing their names are inside. For most of us, there are few greater satisfactions than knowing we are part of a great product.

Inspiring by Being Personally Involved

When I joined Apple, Steve had already come to a keen understanding that people become motivated when their manager or leader makes a direct, active, personal connection to the product. He found that's the best way to inspire others.

His goal is to pump enough energy so that every person in the organization becomes as motivated as he is. They have to feel they are part of the product for this to happen. In Steve's organization, the product is at the core of everything—including recognizing and motivating people. Everyone's attention is focused on the product.

He knows that you have to *become* the product to lead well. He finds powerful ways to make certain every employee is convinced that he knows their contribution is essential to the product's success. This is leadership *by example*. People become very connected to what they are doing—creating the product—because they see how connected their leader is.

Later on, when the Mac came out, though it didn't do well at first, everyone on the team understood its potential. Steve made sure of that, and his enthusiasm never flagged. He is always able to say the right words to keep people fired up over their work. And even with the stress and challenge of working with a leader whose passion for detail and obsession with detail never ends, people love working at Apple—and working for Steve.

The result? Apple had a 3 percent employee turnover rate, the lowest in the tech industry. Even those who rarely saw Steve face to face were loyal to him.

That loyalty is reflected in how people are rewarded for their efforts. The vast majority of companies offer rewards in the form of salary, bonuses, and stock options. This is the case at Apple as well, but Steve is also great at recognizing and rewarding people in different kinds of ways. Money and stock aren't the only keys to keeping people highly motivated.

In the early days especially, whenever a team reached an important milestone, everyone knew there was likely to be some kind of recognition.

The Mac team had a stash of champagne bottles that they broke out whenever somebody felt some small but significant goal had been achieved—something somebody had been struggling with finally worked.

When any member of the Mac team merited a bonus, Steve would pick up the check in a white envelope, walk it over to the employee's workstation and deliver it in person. One day he handed out medals to the Mac team engineers, just to show how much he appreciated their efforts.

And Steve knew that milestones keep people reaching—the software for the screen display has to be working by the fifteenth . . . 75,000 units need to be out the door by the twenty-first. Achieving each milestone was a time to pause and celebrate.

Once the first Macs were on sale, Steve wanted to let the factory workers know that their efforts were appreciated. How does a CEO give recognition? Maybe have Human Resources print out certificates to hang on the wall? Tell the factory manager to hold an "attaboy" meeting?

Not Steve. He went to the factory himself, taking me along. He personally handed out a hundred-dollar bill to every worker, and looked every one of them in the eye as he did it. But the money wasn't the point. What made a profound impression was that the CEO cared enough to hand out the "well done" bonuses *in person*.

One day I was with Steve on one of his "management-by-walking-around" sorties, and we went to the shipping area of the Mac factory. Steve didn't think the products were being prepared for shipment fast enough or well enough. Once again he slipped into the role of imagining himself as the product and describing what he was experiencing as a Mac arriving in the area for shipment. In front of all the shipping people, he went through getting packaged and shrink-wrapped as a way of thinking through how it could be done better and faster.

Most of the people in the shipping area were dumbfounded and obviously uncomfortable with the performance—but it actually revealed ways to increase the flow of shipping. And when he was finished, they all cheered and clapped. We then ordered some pizza and drinks and all celebrated the better shipping method together.

In the end, those changes made it possible to meet the goal he had set of having a Mac shipped every twenty-seven seconds.

After the launch, when we returned to Bandley Drive, we found a large truck at the back door. There were a hundred Macintoshes inside and Steve handed them out himself in a little ceremony, calling out each person's name, shaking hands, and extending his personal thanks.

Each of those Macs was personalized with a plaque bearing the recipient's name. I still have the Mac Steve gave me that day, and I bet most of the ninety-nine other people do, too.

When the iPhone was introduced, *every* employee received one free. So did every part-timer and consultant who had been with the company for more than a year.

Steve was the greatest cheerleader any team could have, continually boosting morale and enthusiasm with lines like, "What we're doing here will send a giant ripple through the universe."

Encouraging the "Artist" in Everyone

Steve is an artist—Apple's "head artist," to use a term that has recently gained currency but was an appropriate description of him from the first.

He encourages his design team to think of themselves as artists as well. He took the entire Mac team on a tour of the Louis Comfort Tiffany Museum in 1982. Why? Because Tiffany was an artist who had successfully made the shift to mass production.

Steve took advantage of the artist sensibility in his engineers. Always in hyper-mode about having new products ready to show, he whips the troops into shape like a lion tamer, with lines like, "Real artists ship on time."

Andy Hertzfeld, a key member of the original Mac design team, put it this way: "The Mac team had a complicated set of motivations, but the most unique ingredient was a strong dose of artistic values. The goal was never to beat the competition, or to make a lot of money; it was to do the greatest thing possible, or even a little greater."

Letting People Know

For some reason, reporters rarely seem to write about one of Steve's most impressive character traits: how much thought he puts into letting people know that they are important and that what they do is critical.

Steve thinks regularly about how to build enthusiasm. He's got a natural talent for it but also makes a point of observing others who have this ability. Exactly what do they say? What is their manner? How do they tell if the other person is listening to what they're saying?

It's easy to lose track of how critical the human element is. Steve is a role model for everyone at Apple, from senior executives to the teams manning the Genius Bars at the Apple Stores. In his much-quoted 2009 commencement speech at Stanford University, he said, "You have to trust in something—your gut, destiny, life, karma, whatever. This approach has never let me down, and it has made all the difference in my life." He instills that same sense of trust, purpose, and vision into the people who work for him.

He was a big supporter of developing an Apple Sabbatical. On reaching five years with the company, the employee would get one month off with pay. But not just for lying on a sunny beach drinking piña coladas: We let each person know he or she was expected to come back with some new ideas about a product, a process, or a broader issue involving the company and its strategy. The sabbatical was to be time to revitalize your creative thinking.

Practicing Hands-On Motivation

Steve is also a master of "management by walking around." You might see him any day of the week, walking the halls, dropping in to ask, "What are you working on?" or "What problems are you having?" Occasionally, I would see him in a more challenging mode demanding, "What are you doing to earn the money I'm paying you?"

To some troops, this can be uncomfortable. They consider it micromanaging. But the approach can also create more positive feelings, leaving people thinking, "He cares not only about the product, he also cares about my role. I'm part of something bigger. We're in this together." Through the years Steve has managed his employees by being ever-present in their lives. He feels that if you are accessible and listen to them, they will rise to meet your expectations.

Andy Grove, then the president of Intel, worked something like this as well, if in a somewhat different way. Intel of course was a much bigger company than Apple at the time. Andy would walk in on people unannounced and they would often feel threatened. But he walked in because he wanted to be part of everything that was going on and instill the spirit of solving problems and constantly looking for better solutions.

This kind of leadership is based on being everywhere at once. If it's done properly, it makes everyone feel part of the whole picture.

Today this hands-on style of management is even more important. With our cell phones, text messaging, and e-mailing the person in the next cubicle, we're being drawn closer by technology while we're growing farther apart from the people in our lives. Yes, Steve uses e-mail extensively but he remains as intense a hands-on manager as ever. Still today, I follow the lessons I learned from him about hands-on management and product development: People in my organizations know I'm available, and that about any issue of significance, I'd rather see them face to face than receive an impersonal e-mail.

When they needed a breather, everyone on the Mac team was drawn to that atrium I described earlier. It was the gathering spot to relax, decked out with video games and stocked with unlimited supplies of his favorite drink, a then-new local product called Odwalla juice. (Steve's well-known preference for Odwalla has made it a huge international success.)

It was a great place for sharing what you were working on, what you needed, what challenges you were facing. A gathering place like the Mac atrium helps everyone get a sense that they aren't alone. A problem facing one part of the team is a problem for everyone.

A Steve Leadership Tactic:
Very Frequent Review Sessions

In addition to the big team retreats that happened every three months in those days, and the impromptu milestone celebrations, there were the "meat-and-potatoes" product review sessions that happened formally every week. Steve believed in *very* frequent product reviews.

Even with all that communicating, he didn't wait for the next review session when an idea or question popped into his head. The leader of a product team would be at dinner, or home with his family, or getting ready for bed, and Steve would call and run down a list of items: "Have you done this, did you get the answer to that, has anybody come up with a candidate for the job you need to fill, have you found a solution to the thus-and-so problem?" And then he might call back a couple of hours later with more items he had thought of—most of them very detailed.

But each time, he would ask, "Can you talk now?" His implied sense that you worked for him twenty-four hours a day was at the same time tempered with showing respect for your private life.

He breaks some of the supposedly ironclad rules about how to handle people. He's notorious for pushing people to their limits and expecting them to work to the extreme every day. Why do they put up with the after-hours interruptions?

It's always tough to work for a perfectionist. You get along if you strive to be as energized, enthusiastic, and inspiring as your leader.

Are Your Employees Using Your Products?

This may not apply in your business: If you manufacture semiconductor chips, or bedsprings, or tractor parts . . . or if you're in a service business designing websites, or delivering packages around town, what I'm suggesting here probably isn't going to do anything for you.

But if you provide products or services that your employees can use, then you want to find effective ways of making sure that your employees are not just users of what you offer, but enthusiastic—using the goods not just because someone is checking up on them but because they believe in the products.

This goes one step further: If I were the head of Intel, for example, I would expect loyal employees to be using computers at home that carried the label "Intel Inside."

In the pre-Mac days, new Apple employees were hired on a trial basis and were expected to learn how to use the Apple II. After three weeks, they were tested. If they hadn't taken the trouble to learn how to use the computer, that was taken as a sign they didn't really care about the product or the company, and they were shown the door.

Pass the test, and Apple gave them an Apple II computer to take home as their own.

In 1985, after the Mac had been introduced, I had my facilities group design an Apple store for employees on nearby Bandley Drive, stocked with Apple products: computers, printers, peripherals, and accessories. This was not a profit center but a way of encouraging employees to keep up with the latest versions of all the hardware. You could walk out with a Mac or an Apple II for about half the manufacturing cost, about 75 percent off retail.

Even better, every employee had the once-a-year privilege of buying a computer for a family member or friend . . . at the same discounted price—another reward for the Macintosh pirates as well as the non-pirates in the rest of Apple.

The company was also very generous with suppliers, developers, and consultants. "Would you like a couple of the new Macs? A Laser-Writer? A server?" The loss to the company was a trickle of revenue, less than a rounding error; the gain in good will and enthusiasm for Apple products was enormous, beyond calculation.

The Grandest Reward

There are few things in the business world of more value than being staffed with people who truly care about the company and its products. Chuq von Rospach, a seventeen-year Apple veteran, put it this way, "I went to work for Apple for simple reasons: It was a company that I felt could make a difference and improve society. Apple is a rare breed of company not afraid to try to improve the world around it." That kind of attitude is what fosters the degree of product-focused success.

One Apple programmer from the early days (he hopes to return, which is why I'm not giving his name) captured the way this attitude permeates the company: "Even two years after I left Apple, I still feel like I celebrate two Christmases—the one with my family, and the one in January at Macworld when Steve Jobs gets up on stage and says: 'I have a few things to show you today that I think you'll really like.'"

As "head artist," Steve always wants to offer a big, headline-grabbing splash, first to the shareholders at the annual corporate meeting and at Macworld, to the near-rabid Apple enthusiasts and developers. He's great at "creating the buzz," within the company and to the world at large. The entire staff stops work when he gives his Macworld speech and gathers to watch on special screens set up in the campus restaurant. Steve knows he's talking to a global audience but it's just as important to him that he's also talking to every Apple employee and contractor—especially those who had a connection, however remote, in creating the products he's introducing that day. (A number of Steve's launch presentations can be seen on YouTube; search for "Steve Jobs Macworld.") Often the greatest reward for Steve's pirates is the thrill of seeing their product introduced with a splash, the kind of splash that Steve is so great at creating.

To the sea-faring pirates of old, the reward was plunder. To pirates of today's best companies, one of the biggest rewards comes when a new product or service they had a hand in is launched with more than just a press release.

Just watch Steve on stage at a launch and imagine the pride and satisfaction you'd be feeling if you had had a role in creating, marketing, or launching it. Then ask yourself what you can do to create the same sense of reward for your own people.

PART III

TEAM SPORTS

The Product-Driven Organization

One of the most critical aspects of any organization is getting it structured right to meet the needs of the business. In the early Apple years, the company flourished with the success of the Apple II. Sales were high and growing exponentially every month, Steve Jobs had become the national poster boy for high-tech and the symbol of Apple products, with Steve Wozniak receiving less than his deserved credit as the technical genius behind it all.

Then, in the early 1980s, the picture began to change, but the management of Apple did not understand and did not see the problems developing. To make things worse, the financial success of the company was masking the problems.

The Best of Times, the Worst of Times

It was a period when the whole country was suffering. In early 1983, times were not favorable for selling much of anything. Ronald Reagan had succeeded Jimmy Carter in the White House, and America as a whole was still climbing out of a nasty recession—a peculiar one in which rampant inflation, usually associated with overheated demand, was combined with depressed economic activity. "Stagflation," it was called. And in order to tame the inflation monster, Federal Reserve Chairman Paul Volcker had driven interest rates sky high, choking off consumer demand.

Closer to home, IBM had landed like a ton of bricks on the little PC sandbox that Apple once had all to itself. IBM was the lone giant among pygmies in the personal-computer business. And the "pygmies" were the likes of General Electric and Honeywell and Hewlett-Packard. Apple couldn't even be called a pygmy. It would have amounted to a rounding error if placed in IBM's P&L statement. Was Apple therefore destined to be flicked away, demoted to the flash-in-the-pan footnotes of business textbooks?

Though the Apple II was the company's cash cow, Steve rightly saw that its appeal would be fading. Worse, the company had just faced its first major failure: the recall of every one of the new $7,800 Apple III machines, due to a problem with a faulty cable that cost less than thirty cents.

Then there was the onslaught by IBM with its unlikely, cutesy "Charlie Chaplin" ads. By its entry, Big Blue had the profound effect of legitimizing personal computing as something more substantial than a hobbyist's playground. The company had virtually created a vast new market with the snap of its fingers. But the immediate question for Apple was: How in the world could it counter the legendary market power of IBM?

To survive, let alone thrive, Apple needed a great Second Act. In the little development group Steve was managing, he believed he had the antidote: the product-driven organization. But he would face one of the only insurmountable hurdles of his career, a challenge he himself was about to be responsible for creating.

Leadership Search

The leadership situation at Apple was shaky. Steve was chairman of the board of directors, a job he took very seriously. Still, his main attention was focused on the Mac. Mike Scott hadn't yet proved to be an effective choice as president, and Mike Markkula, the angel investor who had put up the initial money to get the two Steves started in business, was still acting as CEO but still looking for a way to turn the job over to someone else.

Despite all the pressures he was under, about once a month Steve drove to the nearby Stanford campus, usually with me for company. On the many car trips I made with Steve, to Stanford and elsewhere, the ride was always an experience. He is a very good driver, very attentive to the road and what the other drivers were doing; but back then he drove the same way he managed the Mac project: in a hurry, wanting everything to happen as fast as possible.

You had a sense that any newcomer could learn a lot about Steve's personality and focus by riding in that Mercedes with him. The newcomer would also quickly discover Steve's love of music, clearly a major part of his life. He'd say, "Have you ever heard this before?" and start a Beatles song or another of his favorites, turned up as loud as on my first trip with him to PARC, so that we practically had to shout to hear each other above the music.

On those monthly Stanford visits, Steve met with students at the Business School—either in a small lecture hall with thirty or forty students, or in a seminar setting, around a conference table. Two of the early students, when they graduated, were hired by Steve into the Mac group: Debi Coleman, and Mike Murray.

At one of Steve's weekly staff meetings with the Mac team leaders, he made some comments about the need for a new CEO. Debi and Mike sprang to life and began to sing the praises of the president of PepsiCo, John Sculley, who had once spoken to their Business School class. Sculley had masterminded the marketing campaign in the 1970s that had finally wrested significant market share from Coca-Cola. Known as the Pepsi Challenge (with Coke, of course, as the challengee), these were ads in which blindfolded consumers tasted the two soft drinks and were asked to say which they liked better. In the ads, of course they always picked Pepsi.

Debi and Mike talked with a burst of enthusiasm about Sculley as this seasoned CEO and marketing genius, and I think everybody present had the sense of "Just what we need."

I assume Steve soon began phone conversations with John. After a few weeks, he spent a long weekend of meetings with John; this would have been in the winter—I remember Steve telling me of being in Central Park with fresh snow on the ground.

Though John of course knew absolutely nothing about computers, Steve was very impressed with his insights into marketing, part of what had brought him to leadership of this giant marketing company that is PepsiCo, and which Steve appreciated could be a great asset to Apple. But for John, there were obvious drawbacks to what Steve was offering. As a company, Apple was miniscule compared to PepsiCo. Besides, all of John's friends and business contacts were on the East Coast. And on top of that, he had been told he was one of three candidates to become PepsiCo board chairman. His first answer was a flat-out no.

Steve has always had a full measure of a trait that is one mark of a successful leader: determination. The capper in his wooing of Sculley came with the line that has become business legend: "Do you want to spend the rest of your life selling sugar water, or do you want a chance to change the world?" The question revealed less about Sculley than what it said about Steve himself—clearly he saw *himself* as destined to change the world.

John remembered much later, "I just gulped because I knew I would wonder for the rest of my life what I would have missed."

The romancing of Sculley continued for several months, but by Spring 1983, Apple Computer finally had its new CEO. Sculley had thereby traded management of a long-established global enterprise, and one of the world's iconic brands, for management of a relatively small company in a field he knew nothing about. A company, moreover, that just the day before yesterday had been two-geeks-in-a-garage and was now up against the titan of the industry.

For the next several months, John got along famously with Steve. The trade press dubbed them "The Dynamic Duo." They took meetings together and, at least during the working day, were practically glued at the hip. More than that, they were a mutual tutoring society—John showing Steve how a major enterprise is managed, Steve inducting John into the mysteries of bits and bytes. Yet right from the beginning, the major attraction for John Sculley was Steve Jobs's master project, the Mac. With Steve as the scoutmaster and tour guide, you wouldn't have expected John's interest to be directed anywhere else.

To help John with the challenging transition from soft drinks to what must have seemed the mysterious world of technology, I put one of my IT employees, Mike Homer, in an office near his, with the assignment of working as his right-hand person to offer technology insight. When Mike left that job, a youngster named Joe Hutsko took over—all the more remarkable because Joe had no college degree and no formal technical training, yet was 100 percent up to the job. I thought for John and for Apple to succeed, having a techie at his sleeve was essential.

Steve went along with these intermediaries but wasn't too happy about it; he would have preferred to be the sole source of John's technology knowledge. But clearly Steve had other things on his mind than being John's tutor.

John and Steve were so much on the same wavelength that they would sometimes complete each other's sentences. (Well, actually I never heard them do that, but the story has become part of the John/Steve legend.) Part of this thinking alike, it turned out, was part of the process of John gradually taking on Steve's view that the Apple future was all about Macintosh.

Neither Steve nor John could have recognized the battle that lay ahead. Even if a modern Nostradamus had predicted a battle, we would certainly have assumed it would be a fight over products: Macintosh versus Lisa, or Apple versus IBM.

It never occurred to us that the battle would be, of all things, about how a company is organized.

The Go-to-Market Maze

Indeed, one big issue for Steve was Apple's own Lisa computer, which the company had rolled out the same month that Sculley was hired. With the Lisa, Apple aspired to crack IBM's stronghold with business customers. At the same time, an upgrade version of the Apple II was also launched: the Apple IIe.

Steve had been insisting all along that the Lisa was built around outdated technologically, but it faced an even bigger hurdle in the marketplace: The starting price was a whopping ten grand. The Lisa had struggled for its footing right out of the gate. Underpowered, overweight, and overpriced, it flopped pretty quickly and was not much of a factor in the coming crisis. Meanwhile the IIe, with new software, better graphics, and improved ease of use, was a resounding success. No one had expected that this more-or-less routine upgrade would turn into a great hit.

The Mac's target, by contrast, was the novice, the individual consumer. Its price would be about two grand—much more attractive than the Lisa's pricing, but still a lot more expensive than its major competitor, the IBM PC. And there was still the Apple II, which, as things turned out, would continue to be around for several more years. So now Apple was the tale of two products, the Apple IIe and the Mac. This is the kind of issue John Sculley had been hired to solve. But how could he, when his ears were being filled with Steve's tales of the Mac and the glories it would bring to computer users and to Apple.

Because of this organizational conflict, the company lined up on two sides, Apple II versus Mac. The same was true in the stores selling Apple products: The biggest competitor for the Mac was the Apple II. At the peak of this conflict, the company had about 4,000 employees, of which 3,000 were in support of the Apple II product line and 1,000 in the Lisa and Mac organizations.

Despite that three-to-one imbalance, most employees viewed John as neglecting the Apple II business because he was so focused on the Mac. But inside the company it was hard to see this us-versus-them as a real problem because, again, it was masked by the huge sales revenues and the $1 billion of cash Apple by then had in the bank.

The growing product portfolio set the stage for some spectacular fireworks and high drama.

The route to market for the Apple II was the traditional one in the consumer electronics business: sold through distributors. The distributors would resell to schools and colleges, and to retailers. As in other businesses—washing machines, soft drinks, cars—it was the retailers who were actually selling the product to individual customers. Apple's customers, in short, were not then individual end-users but large distribution organizations.

In hindsight, it's clear that this was the wrong sales channel for a technology consumer product like the Mac.

As the Mac team worked feverishly on final cleanup of last-minute items for the much-delayed launch, Steve took a demo model on the road for a pre-launch press tour visiting eight or so cities across the U.S. to give media people a sneak preview of the computer. At one stop, the demo didn't go so well. There was some kind of glitch in the software.

Steve did his best to cover it up. As soon as the reporters had left, he called Bruce Horn, who was responsible for that piece of the software, and described the problem.

"How long will it take?" Steve asked.

After a moment, Bruce told him, "Two weeks." Steve knew what that meant: It would take anybody else a month, but Bruce was the kind of guy who would lock himself in his office and pretty much stay there until he had the problem licked.

Yet Steve knew taking that long would cripple the launch schedule. He said, "Two weeks is too much."

Bruce explained what was involved.

Steve respected Bruce and knew he was giving a valid assessment. But he said, "I understand what you're saying but you've got to get it sooner."

I never really understood where this came from or how he developed it, but Steve has acquired the ability, even lacking the technical knowledge, to assess accurately what's possible and what isn't.

There was a long pause while Bruce thought this through. Then he said, "Okay, I'll try to get it done in a week."

Steve let Bruce know how pleased he was. When he's pleased and grateful, you can hear the twinkle of enthusiasm in his voice. Moments like that are *so* motivating.

Virtually the same situation came up again as the launch date approached, when the team of software engineers developing the operating system hit a snag. With one week left before the code had to be delivered for disk duplication, Bud Tribble, the head of the software team, told Steve they weren't going to make it. The Mac would have to be shipped with buggy, unstable software labeled "demo."

Instead of the expected explosion, Steve offered ego massage. He lauded the design team as the greatest. All of Apple was counting on them. "You *can* make it happen," he said, in that irresistible tone of encouragement and certainty.

And then Steve ended the conversation before the programmers had a chance to argue. They had been putting in ninety-hour weeks for months, often sleeping under their desks instead of going home.

But he had inspired them. On the last day, literally with only minutes to spare, they got it done.

Noticing Signs of a Conflict

Early signs that the sweetness and light between John and Steve might be dissipating, however, came in the long lead-up to the advertising blitz that would mark the introduction of the Macintosh. This is the story of the famous Macintosh sixty-second TV commercial for the 1984 Super Bowl broadcast, directed by Ridley Scott, who had just become one of the hottest directors in Hollywood for his *Blade Runner*

For those not already familiar with it, the Macintosh ad depicted a packed auditorium filled with drone-like workers in suits and ties staring fixedly at a giant screen, where a sinister figure was lecturing to them— suggestive of a scene from George Orwell's classic novel, *1984*, about a government controlling the minds of its subjects. Suddenly an athletic young woman in T-shirt and red shorts came running in, running down the aisle, and hurling a sledgehammer at the screen, shattering it. Sunlight broke into the room, fresh air wafted in, and the workers snapped out of their trancelike state. A voiceover declared: "On January 24th, Apple Computer will introduce Macintosh. And you'll see why 1984 won't be like *1984*."

Steve loved the commercial the moment the ad agency screened it for him and John. John was apprehensive, though. He thought the ad was crazy. Still, he allowed that "it just might work."

When the board of directors saw the commercial, they *hated* it, and gave instructions for the ad agency to be told to contact the network about canceling the Super Bowl time slot that Apple had purchased, and getting Apple's money back.

The network presumably made an honest effort but reported back that they couldn't find a buyer.

Steve Wozniak clearly remembers his own reaction. "Steve [Jobs] called me over to show me the ad. After watching it, I said, 'This ad is us.' I asked if we were going to show it on the Super Bowl and Steve said that the board had voted against it."

When he asked why, the only part of the response Woz remembers focusing in on was that the ad would cost $800,000 to run. Woz says, "I pondered this for a second and said that I'd pay half of it if Steve would pay the other half."

In hindsight, Woz says, "I realize now how naive I was. But at the time I was very sincere."

It turned out not to be necessary in any case because, rather than see a lackluster Macintosh replacement ad run, Apple's executive vice president of sales and marketing, Fred Kvamme, at the last minute made the critical call that wrote a page in the history of advertising: "Air it."

When the ad ran, viewers were fascinated and stunned: They had never seen anything like it. That evening, television station news directors all over the country decided the ad was so unique that it was newsworthy, and reran it as part of their nightly news programs, giving Apple millions of dollars worth of additional advertising, *free*.

Once again Steve had been right in following his instincts. Early the morning after the ad had run, I drove with him past a computer store in Palo Alto, where we found a long line of people waiting for the doors to open. The story was the same at computer stores all around the country. Today many laud that ad as the best TV commercial ever aired.

Yet within Apple, the ad was damaging. It only stoked the flames of envy that people in the Lisa and Apple II groups felt toward the upstart Macintosh. There are ways to dissipate this kind of product envy and jealousy within a company, but they can't be addressed at the last minute. If Apple management had recognized the problem, they could have worked on making everyone in the company feel proud of the Mac and passionate about its success. No one understood what the friction was doing to the workforce.

Leadership Frictions

Before the public ever saw a Macintosh in real life, Steve held an all-employees meeting. There had been plenty of buzz, but no one in the company other than those on the Mac team had ever seen the actual computer. David Arella, the HR worker I had hired despite his lack of appropriate experience, lights up when he talked about that Mac intro. "Steve gave one of the most rousing speeches I ever heard. He made us feel, 'I'm at the right place at the right time.' It was the most telling speech I've ever heard," he says. But it was a single meeting, at the very last minute—too late to make a difference to the rival forces within the company.

Two days after the Super Bowl, the Apple ad was still the talk of the entire country when Steve, decked out in a navy-blue double-breasted jacket and polka-dot tie, stepped onto the stage and gave one of those celebrated new-product intros that would become his hallmark. Smiling his impish smile, he uncovered a Mac and invited it to speak. And it did speak, saying, "Hello, I am Macintosh. Never trust a computer you cannot lift. . . . I'm glad to be out of that bag." And then it said, "It is with considerable pride that I introduce a man who has been like a father to me—Steve Jobs."

The audience *roared* its approval of Steve and its fascination with a computer unlike anything they had ever seen.

John Sculley and I were standing in the wings when Steve finally came off the stage and said something like, "This is the proudest moment of my life." We knew what he meant: He had not just introduced a computer, he had introduced a whole new way of computing. He was elated.

Being the Public Face of Your Product

The product-driven organization has the product as the most important element in everything it does. Steve is a towering example of being the face of your product wherever you go. The most obvious place to witness this is when he is about to make a presentation at a press conference or Mac Expo. Steve often pays little attention to the prepared remarks. At the same time, he is always fiercely demanding about the smallest detail—down to the exact placement on stage of the key product being introduced, exactly how it will be lighted, and on exactly what cue it will be revealed.

To watch him on stage at one of these presentations was to see a consummate actor; no, in fact, he was better than a great actor, because actors mouth words written by others, while Steve would speak *impromptu*, knowing in advance of course precisely what messages he wanted to get across, yet not following any script. He could hold a huge audience spellbound like this for an hour or even for two.

He is always in hyper-mode about having new products ready to show. No matter what the product, his confidence in it is unparalleled. And he is remarkably imperturbable: When he was introducing Apple's first laser printer, the LaserWriter, he went through his lengthy build-up, finally pressed the button on the computer keyboard to give the print command . . . and nothing happened. Steve went right on talking as if this was the way he had planned it while a gaggle of white-coated techies flocked to the stage, found a loose cable, plugged it in, and vanished.

Steve returned to the computer, pressed the button, and the pages began pouring out. He was not the least bit flustered.

When he introduced the iPhone 4 and could not get a signal, he simply requested that the audience turn off their iPhones, and voilà, with the interference problem solved, he got the signal.

After the Mac introduction, sales jumped off to a nice start. Steve had defined success as selling 50,000 units in the first hundred days. In fact it turned out to be over 70,000, and sales continued to ramp up. June alone saw sales of over 60,000.

But that was the high-water mark. Then came a steady decline in sales, which became steadily more worrisome. The lack of expandability, the small memory capacity (128 kilobytes versus 1 megabyte in the Lisa), the tiny number of available applications at a time when independent software developers were cranking out dozens of nifty applications for the IBM PC—these began to take their toll. A general industry-wide slump in PC sales (IBM clones were now in the mix, too) added to the trouble. The consuming public had decided to pause and take a rest to digest all that the PC revolution had wrought in just a few years.

Steve was alarmed that something was very wrong about sales and distribution. The answer wasn't hard to find: The Mac had no expansion slots for add-on devices, so there were no peripherals for retailers to sell. The computer was for the most part intuitive, so the retailers couldn't make money by selling customer training. But the margins on computers were slim; computer stores made most of their profits from selling the peripherals and training.

The retailers found the Mac to be useful for drawing customers into their stores—everybody wanted to see this radically new type of computer. But once the customer had seen the Mac, the sales rep would tell them all the reasons they should consider an IBM or clone—with price being a strong motivation for the customer to turn his or her back on the Mac.

Another sign that the sales system was wrong: We ran an incentive program for store sales people—sell the most Macs in your store and earn a free Mac for yourself. I'm embarrassed to admit this was my idea; the result was no increase in sales but a 30 percent turnover in store sales staffs—because people were taking the job for the free Mac, and leaving as soon as they had earned it.

Meanwhile, fissures between Steve and John were becoming crevasses.

When Disagreements Escalate to Blowups

After the Macintosh launch, Apple staged a huge worldwide sales meeting at a hotel on Waikiki Beach in Hawaii. The event was a stunning success, but it didn't go unnoticed that John and Steve seemed to have spent almost their entire time at the conference without speaking to each other.

Steve was already at the beginning of an understanding that would grow in him through the years ahead: The IBM PC was billed as a "personal" computer but the truth was different. It was really designed for corporate customers to put on their employees' desks.

And the same for the Lisa. The $10,000 price tag alone announced that it wasn't for the home user.

The Macintosh was different. Alone in a crowded field, it was truly designed for the consumer.

Yet Apple had just hired a new in-house sales force of 2,500 people to sell the Macintosh to *businesses*. Steve was frustrated that he couldn't convince John this was taking Apple in the wrong direction. At dinner the first night in Hawaii, the two had a big blowup; it was like a public announcement that they were no longer the joined-at-the-hip buddies they had been in the early months after John's arrival.

New Ideas Can Sooth
Frictions or Ignite Them

Steve's burning vision of selling to the consumer was the reason he grew so enthusiastic over a visitor to Apple not long after the Hawaii meeting.

Always eager to improve his management skills, Steve had asked me how he could pick the brain of more seasoned corporate leaders, which led me to set up what I called the Management Leadership Program. I invited CEOs to come to Cupertino to sit down and just talk with us—dinner with Steve and me one evening, and the next day a kind of seminar with the visiting CEO for our whole executive staff. Several prominent executives, such as Chrysler's Lee Iacocca and Fred Smith of Federal Express were among those who took us up on the invites, all with perspectives and insights that Steve gobbled up.

One of the people I invited was Chrysler CEO Lee Iacocca. When I called him, he said, "I would love to attend, but how many Dodge vans does Apple lease?"

I said I didn't know but would find out. A couple of days later I called him back and told him what I'd learned: We had none.

Lee said, "Okay, lease four Dodge Vans and I'll come."

It was the first time in my life that I had had a prominent CEO act as a salesman for a few of his company's products. But I rented the vans, and he came.

Lee's visit with Steve was a classic meeting of two historic entrepreneurs. They were almost like twins— the enthusiasm, product focus, and excitement were contagious.

In one of the conversations Steve was having with Lee, the question of organization came up. With Steve running the Mac group as his own fiefdom, Apple was operating like two separate companies. Lee's advice was that a company has to be absolutely product focused.

"At Chrysler," he said, "it's all about the product. In meeting me, you are meeting a Dodge Van." Lee felt that the Japanese car makers were the ultimate of product focus. U.S. companies, in his view, were mired down in structured, top-heavy layers of management.

"Successful companies need to learn from the start-up mentality that innovates." This advice also rang true from our experiences with Steve's much-admired Sony, one of the most product-centric companies you could find, despite having literally hundreds of products. Lee recognized that Sony products showed the same kind of detail and quality that Steve's product did.

It made me realize more clearly than ever another of Steve's principles: that the organization structure of any company needs to be constantly reviewed to make sure it meets the product needs, from development to sales. Apple wasn't doing that.

At the end of the session, I couldn't help wondering whether Steve and Lee might not have had a great working relationship together. *Perhaps, I thought, a relationship that would have worked better than Steve and John Sculley.* Because their business values were so much alike—something that no one would ever claim for Steve and John—I could imagine the two of them bouncing ideas off each other. It wouldn't matter that Lee's background was in a completely different kind of business; the only thing that would matter was that they both had an instinct for how to run a business and how to please their customers. And they each had respect and admiration for the other.

So I know that the answer to my question is, "Yes, Steve and Lee shared the same belief system and would have made a great team." I believe they could even have succeeded as co-CEOs.

It was Fred Smith, though, who had the biggest impact on Steve. He held out the possibility of cutting the Gordian knot that kept the Mac a prisoner of the traditional sales and distribution system. In late 1984, at dinner with Steve and me the night before his appearance at our leadership session, Smith mentioned to Steve that IBM was considering a groundbreaking approach to selling PCs, one that Apple might also consider: a direct-to-consumer system, with factory-to-doorstep shipment using Federal Express.

Steve's eyes lit up. He immediately envisioned having an air strip for Federal Express planes built alongside the Mac assembly plant in Fremont, and Macs rolling off the assembly line and being flown off to the Federal Express hub, then going directly from there to delivery to each individual purchaser the very next day. No more expense of millions of dollars worth of product tied up in the distribution channel. No more retailers pushing competitive products on people who came in to see the Mac.

Steve talked it up excitedly to John. But John, for whom the distributor-retailer system was the natural law of the universe, found the idea strange. He didn't like it. Didn't see how it could work. He nixed it.

What I did not recognize at the time is something that I now believe Lee Iacocca, Fred Smith, and even Ross Perot (more on him later) all clearly saw: The real issue here was who should have been running Apple as its CEO. You can already anticipate my own answer: Steve.

Many people who become highly successful have mentors, especially early in their careers. Part of my goal in starting the Management Leadership Program was in hopes that Steve would find a highly experienced corporate leader he would want as a mentor. It never happened.

But one of the people Steve occasionally talked about in admiring terms—besides Gutenberg and Henry Ford—was Edwin Land, the inventor of the Polaroid camera that in about sixty seconds could spit out a hard-copy color print of a picture you had just snapped. Like Steve, Land was a college dropout, quitting Harvard after one year. Also like

Steve, he was a great innovator. Unlike Steve's other heroes, though, Land was still alive and active. Once when Steve mentioned Land, I suggested he go meet with him.

And he did.

When he returned, he was pumped with excitement. He felt Land was a true American hero. At the same time, Steve felt Land had never received the recognition he deserved because consumers bought his cameras but never really recognized the brilliance of the science behind his products—discoveries that Land had made from his own research. (During one early period, he used to sneak into the Columbia University labs at night, because he couldn't afford lab space of his own.)

It was clear to me that Steve felt sorry for the fate of this brilliant man. More than that, the experience of hearing Land's story had been a learning experience for Steve: It had steeled him with the determination not to let Mac or himself suffer a similar fate.

About a month later, inspired by Steve's enthusiasm, I went to see Land myself, meeting in a restaurant near the Commons in Boston. I found him to be a very Steve Jobs type: little formal education but brilliant and incredibly interesting to talk to on any subject. And I found him to be a man of quality. He had obviously thought the same of Steve—impressed with what Steve had achieved in launching and building Apple, and in the innovative ideas he had talked about for the Mac.

Taking a Stand in a Time of Stormy Weather

But the inspiration of Edwin Land didn't offer any help with the troubles that were beginning to boil up at the top of Apple. As long as John was supporting the Macintosh, Steve wasn't going to pay much attention to the corporate structure issues. But I knew he had been right in those early conversations about the whole of Apple changing from a functional organization to a product-based organization. The company needed to be product-driven.

Taking up Steve's theme, I talked to John many times, trying to get him to understand that the split in the company's operations and focus was wrong.

He listened but I never managed to convince him.

Steve was notably buoyant when George Orwell's year came to a close and 1985 opened. Mostly it was because he had managed to get a number of new applications written for the Mac by third-party developers. The applications were in fact cool and exciting, but too little, too late: It wasn't enough to boost the flagging sales. To Andy Hertzfeld, Steve "seemed oblivious to the slowing sales, and continued to behave as if the Macintosh was a booming, unqualified success. His lieutenants in the Macintosh division had to deal with a growing reality gap, reconciling the ever-changing audacious plans for world domination emanating from their leader with the persistent bad news from the sales channel." They still shared Steve's certainty that the Macintosh defined the future of the personal computer, while recognizing, as Steve couldn't, that the initial version of the Mac they had introduced to the marketplace needed improvements before the sales curve would turn sharply upward.

Steve was trying to figure out how to get the company right and how to get the teams to rediscover their passion. If he wasn't having success, that left it in the hands of the Human Resources VP: me.

In March I organized a major offsite meeting at the Parajo Dunes Hotel to address the growing frictions between the Mac group and the Apple II group, as well as the growing frictions between Steve and John. Ever since, I've referred to this as "the shelf-space meeting."

When the session started, I discovered John had changed the agenda I had put together. He was going to use the meeting as a forum for presenting his own ideas on how to solve the Mac sales issues. John spent four hours trying to convince everyone that the only road that would lead to improved Mac sales was that same approach he had used to make Pepsi so successful: controlling shelf space.

His conclusion was that Apple needed to do a better job of shelf control to get sales going again. Of course that never happened. And my attempt to bring the major organizational issues to light and begin a new Apple got nowhere.

The brewing storm finally broke out as a torrent around the end of May, when John Sculley told Steve that the Macintosh group was no longer his to run. Instead he was being "promoted" to a position with greater overall responsibility; as best I can recall, the title was to be chief technology officer.

The board in fact had been anxious to find an appropriate role for Steve, to keep his remarkable visionary instincts within the company, but they felt he was too temperamental, too inexperienced, for running a product group. John, too, wanted Steve to stay; he just did not want him to continue running the Mac division.

It's time to correct the record: The accepted version of this says that John (or the board) *fired* Steve, or told him he had to leave. That's not the way it happened.

Steve walked out the door of Apple that day, got into his Mercedes, and drove away, deeply hurt. Yes, he could be difficult, but look at the results. The Macintosh was *his* creation. The sales weren't good but they would be getting better. And the rest of the computer industry would be falling all over themselves to offer a mouse, icons, pull-down menus, and all the rest.

But the Mac group had been taken away from him.

John was so upset on hearing Steve had left, that he himself left that day, as well. The difference was that John was back at his desk the next morning—very early, as usual.

Despite a few initial efforts by John to woo him back, Steve would be an Apple outsider for the next ten years. With Steve out of the way, John reorganized the company, making it even more a functional structure. The Macintosh team was no longer a stand-alone, self-contained unit but instead was rolled into becoming part of a new product development group under Del Yocam, a VP who as far as I ever knew had little experience with product development.

It would be easy to see this episode as essentially a battle for control between two executives. But it was far more: It was an object lesson in what happens when a company does not have a cohesive product strategy and is organized functionally instead of in distinct product groups.

The iLeadership principles offered in this book didn't come to me gradually over time through the years. With the background of IBM and Intel, I had been soaking up from the first the basic business principles that Steve was beating the drum for: the product-based organization, as well as building products for and marketing to the consumer, not to business.

Steve's dream of making Apple a product-driven company was dead. Over the coming decade, the company would suffer badly for a variety of reasons; not being organized around products was a leading one of those reasons. Though Steve's thinking was way ahead of most business people at the time, the problem was that he knew what he wanted but didn't yet know how to express it and didn't have the clout to force his ideas on Steve's own handpicked CEO, John Sculley.

Apple would remain a company not organized around product groups until Steve's return.

I realized from watching all this that learning how to make yourself understood, learning how to be persuasive, is critical for a business leader. The only way to ensure a product-driven focus is to have that philosophy made real in the company's organization itself.

And for Steve himself—what next?

Maintaining Momentum

Virtually every entrepreneur, every business manager, and every company goes through a crisis sooner or later. Regardless of size—from the single person trying to build a business to the largest global corporations and their leaders—there will inevitably be turning points when the problems seem overwhelming and nearly insurmountable.

In Steve's handbook, every opportunity starts with an unmet need. If you can build a product to meet that need, it becomes a "must-have." Steve had seen the work Woz was doing as that kind of opportunity. If properly designed and brought down in size and cost, computers would become "must-haves" for a lot of people, not just people who fit the geek profile of Homebrew Computer Club types, but people like himself.

Steve has always realized that when you want something passionately, you have a vastly improved power for convincing others as well.

The product-driven entrepreneur goes from product to product. "So does everyone in business," some will say. But while the product-driven person is always thinking of the next product for the market, most everyone else in business is thinking in terms of the next personal opportunity. And if that means jumping from company to company, no problem.

John Sculley came from a company where "the next product" meant more of the same. At Apple, he was thinking in terms of the next opportunity, not the next product. Mark Hurd, the ex-CEO of HP, went through three companies in eight years—but never developed a product. That's not the exception. Stop and think about it: It's quite common for leaders at traditional companies.

Remaking a Company . . . the Wrong Way

In the fall of 1985, Steve Jobs, the ultimate product guy who didn't want to bounce from company to company, was in crisis mode. Being worth $200 million didn't take away the sting that he was no longer with the company he cofounded. The Macintosh project he so deeply believed would change the nature of computing had been suddenly snatched away from him.

Personally, I wasn't just devastated seeing Steve leave Apple; I was afraid that other top engineers would leave to join him, which would have a crippling impact on Apple's product development. John regretted seeing him leave, as well; all of the Apple execs and board members heard that from John himself at the time, and years later he acknowledged it publicly.

At the same time, I knew I needed to stand up for what I believed and decided to tell some Apple board members they were making a huge mistake. I started with Mike Markkula and spent about an hour on the phone expressing my position: The Mac group needed to be spun out as a separate company headed by Steve. His reaction was that Steve was "too immature."

I met with Arthur Rock at his very dark office in San Francisco. Arthur thanked me for coming, listened to my position, made very few comments, but said he would take my suggestions into consideration in the board's deliberations of what to do. I flew down and met board member Henry Singleton in his LA office. His reaction was about the same as the other two.

A couple of days later, Steve invited me up to his house in Woodside to have lunch. He was living in a 15,000-square-foot house, which as far as I ever saw was mostly unfurnished, and he seemed to actually use only a small portion of it. The meal—a salad with hummus, appropriate to his Buddhist habits—was prepared and served by his cook/housekeeper. The invitation was apparently a way of saying thank you.

He said he really thought my going to the board would help them make the right decision.

John Sculley called a meeting aimed at getting all the Apple VPs to pledge their loyalty to him as CEO. I refused and instead pledged loyalty to Apple, its employees, and shareholders.

John summoned me to his office a few days later and said, "Tell me why I shouldn't fire you. You told several board members I was making a big mistake about Steve." I replied that I thought the disagreement between him and Steve was ridiculous. Plus Apple was two companies, Apple II and Mac, but it was Mac that was the future of the company, and it was Steve's vision that had created the Mac. John needed to find a way to manage the Apple II for the remainder of its technological life, and let Steve get Mac ready to take over the market.

John didn't fire me and instead asked my help in keeping Apple together. I told him, "If one messiah is gone, you can bring back the other one. Call Steve Wozniak. Get him involved again." He actually did, which for a time gave Apple employees more hope about the company's future.

• • •

As for convincing the board, I had been fighting an uphill battle. Steve never played office politics—it just wasn't in his genes or his jeans. John, the CEO with the proven record in business, an executive trusted by Wall Street, was an easy decision for the board. Sure, Steve was co-founder, but he wasn't polite and deferential, and there were no guarantees that the Macintosh would turn out to be all that Steve was claiming for it. Sales were far below what he had projected. And Sculley and the board weren't canceling the Mac anyway. If the Mac had promise, some other Apple manager could take the reins and keep it alive.

So I didn't change the mind of any of the board members—or at least, not enough of them to make a difference.

Steve had grown Apple from nothing into a $2 billion company that ranked 350 in the Fortune 500. And on the strength of the Mac, the company grew five times bigger while he was gone. But he still feels what happened during that time caused Apple a lot of harm, particularly to the Apple product loyalists.

The problem, as Steve put it in an oral history interview for the Smithsonian Institution, wasn't the rapid growth but the change in values. Making money became more important to Apple than the product. The new management was applying standard business practices to a product-driven company that thrived on uniqueness and innovation.

It's true that Apple made incredible profits for about four years, but the new focus finally cost rather than benefited the company. Steve felt Apple should have gone for reasonable profits while focusing on a great product to increase market share, and that this strategy would have given the Mac a third or more of the personal computer market. Instead, computers running Microsoft Windows took over.

Recovering from Disaster

Steve sold all but one share of his Apple stock, changing his balance sheet from a net worth of $200 million to $200 million, less taxes, in his pocket. He told me he had no particular plans but was thinking he might want to become a world traveler, just kicking around from place to place. And then he boarded a plane for Italy.

Over the next weeks, Apple employee and Steve's personal friend Susan Barnes Mack kept calling him, bugging him to come back, telling him that his people were unhappy without him.

Steve wasn't capable of living a do-nothing life. He called one day after six or eight weeks to say he was back.

He thanked me again for the way I had stood up for him by arguing his case to the board members. I hadn't done it for him but because I thought his staying was vital to the future of Apple.

He had a plan in mind, and he was serious. "Let's make one more try at convincing the board members to change their minds. I'm gonna have T-shirts made up that say, 'We want our Jobs back.'"

Damn, I thought. *That's really clever.*

He said, "You get all the employees out for a lunchtime rally and hand out the shirts."

Oops.

I told him, "No, Steve, I'm an Apple executive. I can't do that."

He said something like, "Well, anyway, it's a good idea."

I agreed.

Staying in the Game

For a time, it looked as if Steve had indeed quit the game. That surprised me—it didn't seem like what I expected from the Steve I knew.

But he hadn't quit. He turned out to be the model of how to act in a time of crisis: Keep charging ahead until you find that new road. He was to show the guts and gumption that marks the product-inspired person.

While traveling, Steve had been thinking about a dialog he had had with Stanford professor and Nobel Laureate Paul Berg, after the two had been seated next to each other at a Stanford dinner for French president François Mitterrand. The professor talked about his vision of a personal computer so powerful that students would be able to conduct virtual experiments too complex to be carried out in a student laboratory on campus. No existing personal computer even came close.

At Apple, Steve had been laying the groundwork for more powerful models of the Macintosh. With the constant progression in faster chips and larger hard drives, maybe the professor's dream computer might be doable.

After his return, Steve paid a visit to Paul Berg and said something like, "We talked about this. I'd like to confirm there really is a strong market in universities for the kind of machine you described."

Professor Berg gave Steve the encouragement he had been hoping before.

The next Apple quarterly board meeting rolled around not long after, on Thursday, September 14. How's this for a strange circumstance: Remember that when Steve asked acting-CEO Mike Markkula to make him VP of product development, and Mike, not wanting Steve to have the power of making the kinds of product decisions that position would bring with it, had instead anointed him as board chairman?

Well, no one had gotten around to changing that. When the board members sat down for their September meeting, guess who was sitting at the head of the table. Right: Steven P. Jobs.

I sat in on most board meetings, and would not have missed this one for anything. The atmosphere was solemn—none of the usual smiling faces and pleasant catching-up chatter. For the past three months, the company had gone through unprecedented layoffs and was grappling with major sales and financial problems. No one knew what to expect.

It seemed to me that every board member was nervous. Or maybe it was something else: The board members had all heard a rumor going around that Steve planned to buy out the company. If he did, would he make decisions that would run Apple Computer into the ground? The board members had the integrity of the company to preserve. And of course they each had enough shares in the company to produce a noticeable change on their personal balance sheets if the company didn't survive.

Company executives presented the usual reports of sales, inventories, and so on. The picture was grim. Sales were still tanking. Apple was clearly in trouble, with no short-term solution in sight. The morale of the company was at an all-time low: It's incredibly painful to watch good friends walking out the door with a box of their personal possessions. And it's painful to wonder constantly, "Am I next?"

After the reports, it was Steve's turn. He had a request to make that took them all by surprise. I won't pretend I remember his words exactly, but the gist was: "I'm going to start my own company. I'm not going to compete with Apple. Mine is going to be a computer for the university market. I want to take a few low-level people with me."

That much I knew already. The next part took me by surprise, as well as all the others: "And I'd like to have Apple invest in my company."

I could almost hear a sigh of relief from every direction. No accusations, no anger, no emotions.

After a few minutes of discussion, the board agreed that John and Steve should get together and see what they could work out.

It was dark outside when we all left the building. The three-hour meeting had lasted until about ten at night.

Steve met with John early the very next day with the names of people who had agreed to go with him to his start-up. The list included some people from the business side, as well as Rich Page, and Dan'l Lewin.

John called to fill me in on the conversation, and said, "Looks like a good deal for everyone."

I tried to explain: These weren't low-level people. Rich had been working on a future Mac that he hoped to provide with a million-by-million pixel screen, plus a very big memory and big hard drive. And Dan'l was key to our education market, in charge of the "Kids Can't Wait" program that donated Apple IIe's to the schools. He also ran the Apple University Consortium, the program that offered major discounts to college faculty and students.

I told John, "Steve had said he wouldn't compete, but these are key people he's taking." Besides presenting a real problem, it would send a strong negative message to the remaining employees.

Eventually a deal was worked out allowing Steve to set up his new company but not to take any additional employees.

Steve started NeXT Computer, Inc.—at first spelled Next—and set to work creating what was for all practical purposes the next generation Macintosh he had wanted to do at Apple. He would show he could do what he told everyone he could: build a great product even outside of Apple's protective umbrella.

When Steve Jobs started NeXT, I thought at the time (after I had begun to get over being upset at his departure), *What other name but "NeXT" could possibly express Steve's business philosophy so well?* Yes, he's restless, but he also knows that things never stand still in business, especially in the technology business.

In recent years, Steve's career has had nothing but a rocketing upward trajectory, but as we've seen, it hasn't been without some serious stumbles along the way. Whatever might be happening at any given time, though, Steve's story has consistently, from the very first, been a saga of one "next big thing" after another.

Still, to be honest, I wasn't sure Steve could succeed. Nobody was, not even Steve himself. He told me he was scared to death.

Creating Products That Reflect
the Principles of the Creator

Who can say which of the following is more remarkable: That Steve would not set foot on the Apple campus for another ten years? Or that the NeXT computer platform would lay the foundation for the new-generation operating system of the Macintosh? Or that while a workstation was designed to sell at a six-figure price point well above the reach of most individuals, it would ultimately redirect Steve toward what would become his ultimate calling—designing for the consumer?

Yet even more important than any of these advances was the corporate culture that he nurtured at NeXT. In what would later become a blueprint for Apple, Steve flattened hierarchies, provided generous benefits, reframed staffers as "members" rather than "employees," and oversaw an open-plan facility that physically embodied what for him was a new way of working. His strong team of technical experts, product managers, and marketing people at NeXT was a direct outgrowth of this unconventional culture. Many of them would later play a big role back at Apple.

I've always considered this period as Steve's "exile to the isle of NeXT," yet it was Steve's substitute Apple. He was keeping alive his vision of the future of the Macintosh. The NeXT computer was going to be the next generation Mac.

Meanwhile, at Apple, Steve was like an invisible presence. Even employees who arrived after he left couldn't help but feel his imprint. One employee, though she never met Steve, put it this way: "I had a sense that it was still his company. There was the same pervasive feeling of pride, energy, and passion, and the Steve Jobs story was kept alive by the many people who had been there under his leadership."

What a goal for us all to aspire to: creating an aura so strong that people who never met us still feel our presence after we've left.

Accepting Unlikely Challenges

It takes guts to be up against a wall and still be willing to take on a new challenge, one that every Business School student would label foolhardy.

While Steve was trying to make the NeXT computer into his dream machine, he came across another powerful computer for a specialty use. And the man who had been paying the bills was looking to unload the whole package: the whole team of people plus the computer technology and the software they had created.

This was the digital graphics animation unit of Lucasfilm, George Lucas's film studio in Marin County, California. Lucas wanted to unload the unit to raise money for his divorce settlement, and Steve talked to him about it. There were other interested parties sniffing around, including corporate mogul and one-time presidential candidate Ross Perot, who had sold his firm, EDS, to General Motors, in a deal that gave him a seat on the GM board. Perot structured a transaction to acquire the Lucas operation in a three-way deal with Philips, EDS, and Lucasfilm. The deal was settled, green lights all around, when Perot, at a GM board meeting, in effect accused GM management of incompetence, which suddenly made him *non grata*. His authority to do deals on behalf of the GM was canceled. Lucas's graphics unit was suddenly up for grabs, and Steve stepped in. To me this made perfect sense; Steve and I had talked about his love for the movies. It seemed a perfect match to combine his talent for technology with movie making. I believe as the years roll by, we'll see Steve involve Apple in this, in a big way.

That graphics unit was, of course, what would come to be known as Pixar; the name was faux Spanish, meant to suggest a meaning of "to make pictures." The unit was headed by two computer animation pioneers from New York, Dr. Ed Catmull and Dr. Alvy Ray Smith. Their goal, their dream from the very first, long before the birth of Pixar, was to create the first feature-length animated motion picture made completely with computers.

A third key member of the team was brilliant former Disney animator John Lasseter, hired to do short films that would show off the ever-widening capabilities of the new animation computer that the unit had been developing. (For some reason, many books and articles on the subject pat Steve on the back for being smart enough to recruit Lasseter, when the credit belongs to the two founders. At the time of Steve's deal, Lasseter was already part of the team.)

A few years earlier, back about the time Steve started running into trouble at Apple, Lasseter had created a sensation at Siggraph, the annual convention of the most prominent computer graphics organization. What won all the praise was a film short, written and directed by Alvy and animated by Lasseter, called *André and Wally B*; incredibly, it was only ninety seconds long.

At the time, the limitations of computer animation were all too obvious. Emotion couldn't yet be conveyed on characters' faces and that made subtle storytelling just about impossible. Computer animation was used for special effects or in short films that featured abstract, kaleidoscopic imagery. But the Smith-Lasseter *André and Wally B* told a story that captured the viewer's emotion; it was far ahead of what anyone else in the industry was doing.

After Steve had capitalized the spinoff of the animation unit from Lucas, he began to realize that neither Ed Catmull nor Alvy Ray Smith had any real interest in computers. They saw them simply as tools for creating digital animation. That was really ironic, because Steve thought he had acquired controlling interest in a computer graphics company, while the founders looked on the computer essentially as just a tool for achieving a more powerful way of telling stories. Steve pursued his goal of finding customers who needed an advanced graphics computer, eventually opening sales offices in seven cities, once again showing himself as a man who does not do things in a halfhearted way.

Part of the challenge for the Pixar team was that computer technology had not advanced far enough to make a computer-generated feature film practical. But each year brought the possibility closer. And each year, Lasseter and his crew would show off the latest advances in the Pixar Graphics Computer and its software by producing a short story-film to show at Siggraph. At the 1986 gathering in Dallas, they premiered *Luxo Jr.*, a milestone in animation history. John Lasseter directed as well as animated the short, whose characters were two uncannily expressive desk lamps, one large and one small. In homage to the triumph of that short film and what it eventually opened up for Pixar, a Luxo-type lamp is still featured in the opening credits of every Pixar feature film.

Luxo Jr. was a technological advance, as usual for Pixar, conveying emotion even better than Pixar's earlier efforts. Computer-animation technology was finally being used in the service of real storytelling.

The six thousand people watching the premiere gave it "prolonged and enthusiastic applause." The film won a Golden Eagle at Washington, D.C.'s CINE film festival, and an Oscar nomination for best animated short—the first computer-animated film to receive this acknowledgment. Even though it didn't win, Ed Catmull still feels that *Luxo Jr.* was Pixar's— and computer animation's—turning point.

Maintaining Momentum in the Face of Failures

Steve's real gift is his ability to refine consumer products. He's a superb editor and polisher whose core philosophy is "less is more." He takes things *out* of over-engineered, complicated products, revealing what really makes them usable and exciting. He also has a great sense of when the timing for a product is right. He's proven again and again that he knows what consumers want. When he's strayed from this, he's gotten in trouble. When he's stayed true to his strengths, he's always come out on top, no matter how great the challenge he was facing.

Steve was certainly in trouble in early 1988. Pixar and NeXT were generating income but it wasn't nearly enough. Given the weak sales of both companies, the amount of cash Steve had to wire-transfer from his bank each month to keep them afloat was becoming unnerving as his net worth continued to shrink. For Pixar alone, though income from licensing the Pixar graphics software, producing television commercials, and sale of Pixar computers (mostly to Disney and government agencies) was covering about half the expenses, Steve was routinely sending wire transfers for $300,000 to $400,000 a *month* to keep the company going.

That spring, Steve sat down with Ed Catmull, Alvy Ray Smith, and a couple of other top Pixar executives for a regularly scheduled monthly operational meeting. The Pixar people had no idea how difficult it was going to be.

Steve made it clear that he was stretched to the breaking point and could no longer afford the same cash outlay. Pixar had to be downsized. The Pixar brass were devastated. The cuts would break apart the crack computer animation team they had built over many years, starting as early as the mid-1970s and acknowledged as the best in the business.

Nevertheless, it had to be. But who would be let go? The discussion was grim and seemed to stretch on interminably. Once it was finally over, Steve got ready to leave the meeting, but Bill Adams, Pixar's VP of sales and marketing, had another important agenda item to talk about.

If Pixar showed up at the next Siggraph without its annual new animated short displaying yet again that the Pixar software could be used to create digital animation significantly better than the previous year, and far better than available from any other company, it was sure to start rumors. People would wonder what was wrong; they'd wonder, "If we buy Pixar software now, will they still be around in a couple of years to continue providing support and upgrades?" Sales would almost certainly be threatened.

Despite the bleak financial picture, funding the new short was critical to Pixar's future. Without it, things would go from bad to much worse.

When Bill and the others were through, Steve just sat there. It wasn't hard to guess what was running through his mind.

Finally he asked if there were anything he could take a look at. There was. John Lasseter had created stunning storyboards that captured the graphical approach and feeling of what he hoped would be Pixar's next project, *Tin Toy*. Steve was duly impressed and after much deliberation made his own agonizing decision to fund production despite his cash-flow problems. It would turn out to be one of the best decisions he ever made.

Every new Pixar short broke new ground. *Tin Toy*'s very considerable novelty at the time lay in convincingly animating its main character, a young tot. Until then, many doubted putting emotional expression into human faces could ever be done. The completed *Tin Toy* proved the doubters wrong. This time the film won Pixar the Oscar for Animated Short.

Two hundred million dollars, his personal Apple-enabled bankroll, sounds like a great deal of money. It *is* a great deal of money. But Steve was seeing that bankroll dwindle at an alarming rate.

If Steve hadn't reached into his own pocket to come up with the production budget for the *Tin Toy* short, what followed afterward could never have happened. The Disney leaders had only very gradually come to believe that computer animation could have a place at the studio responsible for *Snow White* and *Cinderella*. After some approaches from Disney execs, the Pixar team showed up for a meeting at the Disney lot in Burbank with a proposal that they produce a Disney-funded one-hour animated television movie.

The Disney people surprised everyone by turning down the TV idea and counteroffering a deal for Pixar to produce a full-length animated feature film.

A series of meetings at the studio led to what Ed Catmull and Alvy Ray Smith had so long dreamed of: Pixar would be producing, for Disney release, the world's first computer-animated full-length feature.

It's a truism that you need always to be prepared for the unexpected. The Pixar team had not anticipated they would be asked for a feature, yet it had been their goal for years.

The very first short concept that Lasseter presented to Disney's Jeffrey Katzenberg carried the working title *Toy Story*. Not much of the original story or characters would end up in the movie, but the title, of course, made it onto the big screen. Katzenberg—the head of Walt Disney Studios under Michael Eisner, CEO of the overall company—could be difficult to work with: He was a tyrant, and even called himself that, virtually bragging about it. But he proved to be a mentor and creative advisor to Lasseter and his team. He'd never say "Do this" or "Do that," but "This isn't working." Screening scenes of the picture, if he thought the story was starting to drag, he'd tell Lasseter, "They're going for popcorn."

During the long months of production—including one span of a few months when Disney ordered a halt until Lasseter and crew could come up with solid solutions to some creative problems, such as the Woody character's being too negative and unsympathetic— costs kept mounting. Eventually the budget overruns topped $6 million. Disney insisted Steve insure the picture's completion by taking out a $3 million line of credit, using his personal assets as collateral.

Steve began to regret the Disney deal; he even started thinking it would have been better if he had never taken on Pixar to begin with.

Because of the cost overruns, the finances of *Toy Story* were beginning to look like a disaster. Unless the picture made more money than any recent Disney animation release, Steve would never get his investment back. In fact it would have to be a box-office smash, taking in at least $100 million, for Steve to see any cash income.

Worse, he now realized why the Disney people had been so eager to retain all the income from the peripherals—the toys, games, dolls, T-shirts, fast-food tie-ins, and the rest. Even if the film itself didn't make any money, Disney might well see a handsome stream of cash flowing in from these other sources. Steve was becoming wise to the ways of Hollywood but the education was looking like it would be costly.

And then, suddenly, it all turned around. Steve's team of first-timers in the big leagues of film-making had proved they did indeed belong in the big leagues. Michael Eisner had decided to postpone the *Toy Story* opening. Instead of the scheduled date, the picture would be Disney's big release for the Christmas holidays.

The capper: Eisner called the film "both a spectacular movie and a lovable movie."

It took some five years from contract signing to premiere for *Toy Story*, but for everyone involved, it had been well worth the struggle and the wait. Many people had been skeptical that a company headed by Steve Jobs, the technologist, could produce a praiseworthy work of art. But those suspicions were based on a misunderstanding. The Pixar deal from the first had been that Steve would be in charge of business dealings, and the original team would have sole and absolute domain over all creative decisions.

After its premiere Thanksgiving week, 1995, the film won great accolades from critics, parents, children—viewers of all kinds, all around the world. A film that eventually cost some $30 million went on to earn $190 million in the U.S. and a total of over $300 million globally. It established the production company, Pixar, as a star in the Hollywood firmament.

As of this writing, in 2010, Pixar is unique among Hollywood studios: It is the only major studio that has never lost money on any production.

And all of this because Steve Jobs, somewhat against his better judgment, was willing to fund those early Pixar short demo films.

During the time *Toy Story* had been in production, the rest of the Pixar team had been focused on two fronts: improving their graphics computer, and continuing to develop their animation software packages. The Pixar Image Computer was a great product for anyone who needed to keep track of large or detailed images as well as documents. Steve was convinced he could make this specialized computer marketable.

But where was the market? First released in 1986, the machine demanded an outlay of almost $200,000 before it would start working. And while it was great at doing what it was supposed to do, it was very difficult to operate, especially for anyone who wasn't already a tech whiz.

The company made a concerted effort to sell the Image Computer into the medical industry. But the doctors and other health professionals who saw the demo almost uniformly decided that it would take too much time to learn to use. Hospital and clinic staffs were already far too busy. Three strikes and you're out: The Pixar computer was too expensive, too hard to use, and had too limited a market. The company had sold fewer than three hundred of the machines. Steve gave up in 1990, selling the hardware business to a company called Vicom for a mere $2 million.

Vicom folded a year later.

By the time Steve's NeXT computer was released, it offered another demonstration of his commitment to creating not just the hardware but the software, as well. He had done that for the Macintosh, and now he had done it again at NeXT, his engineers building the unique NeXTStep operating system.

Two years later Steve introduced a more advanced machine, the NeXT Cube. Both the original machine and the Cube were expensive, specialized workstations aimed primarily at the academic market and high-end users.

Like all great entrepreneurs, Steve is a master juggler who's almost always working on several apparently unrelated projects at once. These next big things have a way of eventually proving part of a unified master strategy, though that didn't apply quite the same when he was running NeXT and Pixar simultaneously.

NeXT was not one of the happier chapters in Steve's career. The NeXT computer was a typically Stevian quantum leap forward that was much lauded and admired but produced less-than-spectacular sales. The machine had much greater storage capacity and a larger, clearer display than the other personal computers of the time, Macs included. Those in the know were enthusiastic, and in fact the first web browser and server were created by Internet pioneer Tim Berners-Lee on a NeXT Cube, in 1991. Quite an impressive pedigree.

Though originally intended to be used in education, the NeXT did sell enough units to be a minor success in a few narrow markets. The man who was in charge of education marketing at NeXT, Burt Cummings, described the NeXT computer this way: "Engineering excellence. There were tight specs for everything on the design. No expense spared. Magnesium casing for the CPU unit, beautiful black finish. State-of-the-art magnetic-optical drive. Fantastic user interface, beautiful operating system, but . . ."

The "but" is that it suffered from two of the same drawbacks as the original Macintosh: It just plain cost too much—some $10,000, much more than the first Macs. Just as bad, if not worse, developers were not stepping forward to create applications for the NeXTStep platform. Part of the reason was again financial. The cost to develop programs under the original NeXTStep system was huge, running, I'm told, to the millions of dollars—much too high in the face of the mediocre sales that meant a software developer who had committed a significant bankroll would not have much of a potential marketplace; the chance of seeing a handsome return on the investment was just too slim.

Burt Cummings's conclusion: "So essentially it was DOA. It was designed for the university market but was just too expensive. It's great to build for beauty, but you need to know your market."

Yet Pixar VP Bill Adams offers another perspective. "If NeXT had been done at Apple, he would have succeeded," because there he would have had the backing of a proven, established company that would have stood behind the product with promotion, advertising, industry connections, and customer confidence. And this wasn't just Bill's opinion; when he raised the issue with Steve, "He admitted as much to me," Bill says.

In time, Steve had simply faced the hard truth that his NeXT computers—despite all the pluses of being fast, with great architecture, and great looks—were too expensive for the companies that coveted them.

It was a bitter pill, but just as he had with the Pixar computer, he closed down the manufacturing of the NeXT machines, turning his focus to selling copies of the NeXTStep operating system software. IBM showed a serious interest in licensing the product to run on their own computers. It looked like the deal that might rescue NeXT. A team of IBMers showed up to present the company's offer to Steve, and shoved a hundred-page contract under his nose. I've been told that he picked it up, dropped it in the trash basket, and told them he didn't sign any contracts longer than three or four pages. Before IBM could come up with a solution to the "three or four pages" edict, the man at IBM who had been championing the project left his post. Nobody else at IBM was interested in Steve's software.

The NeXT and Pixar stories are remarkably similar. Steve was known for his work building computer hardware but had struck out twice. The graphics computer developed at Pixar was a product aimed at the business market. When he first purchased the company, Steve hadn't yet fully realized that his real strength is consumer products, not business hardware.

Ironically, Pixar ended up as a company that produced consumer products—animated motion pictures—even though this direction may not have always been clear. It was transformed from a small digital graphics services company into an entertainment business, one of the great success stories of recent decades. Maybe in this case Steve just stumbled onto his next big thing through sheer luck. But, as always, luck favors the prepared. As things evolved, Pixar reshaped the entertainment industry, and what Steve wasn't able to see at first he most certainly grasped in due course.

Finding an Entrepreneurial Style

That Lasseter and Katzenberg were able to work successfully together serves as a reminder: No two entrepreneurs are alike; each has his own personal style, and conflicting styles *can* mesh.

True entrepreneurial leaders are always looking over the horizon for the next opportunity. It is this quest that keeps them going and sometimes they find their true mission along the way, as Steve did.

I've always been fascinated by the differing styles of people who build great enterprises. I once approached the founder of JetBlue Airlines about using a product I had developed that would allow keeping pilots' laptops in sync with the database used at the airport for route information, weather, etc.

I was drawn to JetBlue because of their creativity: I felt they had re-defined air travel. (In fact, they spoiled me early on; I will no longer travel without a TV at my seat.)

When I met JetBlue founder David Neeleman, I recognized him as very much a Steve Jobs type. He had previously started Morris Air, sold it to Southwest Airlines, then had a falling out with Southwest CEO Herb Kelleher; Neeleman, like Steve Jobs, was sent packing.

He then founded JetBlue, but in 2007 got ousted by the board.

So what happens to entrepreneurs who have these kinds of setbacks?

They get up and start over again. David has started a new airline in Brazil, "Azul" (it means *blue* in Portuguese), which logged 2.2 million passengers in its first twelve months, shattering the previous record for a start-up airline.

Why in South America? Because they have one of the fastest-growing economies in the world. As David puts it, "What matters isn't what happens to you in life. What really matters is how you react to it."

One of the key elements of the entrepreneur is momentum a characteristic that I see in all of these leaders. Do not quit, keep it going, always going forward despite the setbacks, always remaining open to the next idea. I learned that from Steve and have held it as a guiding principle, a principle that had led me to create more than ten products in the last eight years.

Martin Luther King once said, "Judge a man on how he reacts to failure, not success."

Recovery

In 1995, Pixar was glowing with the success of *Toy Story* but NcXT was still on life support, only surviving because Steve continued to pour huge amounts of money into it every month. Yet his business life was about to turn around in a most remarkable way, which would lead to his becoming acknowledged as perhaps the best CEO ever.

When you consider what his younger years were like, his success is almost laughable, making clear that no one who gets off to a bad start or a late start should ever lose hope about what could lie ahead for them.

Recognizing Opportunities

In 1971, a mutual neighborhood friend brought Steve Jobs, then sixteen, over to see the handiwork of a neighborhood kid, Steve Wozniak. Three years earlier, at age eighteen, Woz had already built his first computer with a friend. In those days "computer" to most people still meant a massive, complex machine housed in its own air-conditioned room and tended by guys in white jackets. The first commercial kits for building primitive home computers wouldn't appear for several years. So even though Woz's version of a computer couldn't do much more than turn some tiny light bulbs on and off, it was still an impressive achievement.

Steve immediately recognized Woz, who was five years older, as a kindred spirit who shared his passion for technology. The two were similar in many ways and very different in others. They turned out to be perfect complements.

From the early grades, Steve Jobs had been something of a troublemaker. Then one teacher, a Mrs. Hill, recognized he was really very bright, and bribed him to buckle down and study, using money, candy, and a camera-building kit. Steve became so motivated that he even ground his own lens for the camera. In the Smithsonian oral-history interview, Steve said, "I think I probably learned more academically in that one year than I learned in my life." Quite a testimonial for how one teacher can change a student's entire history.

That experience shaped Steve in a way that will come as a surprise to many people. From the very earliest days of Apple, he set up programs that provided ways for students and teachers—from elementary school all the way through university—to purchase computers at a very steep discount. This wasn't some public relations gimmick; it was a reflection of a deeply held belief growing out of his own childhood experience in Mrs. Hill's classroom:

I'm a very big believer in equal opportunity. . . . Equal opportunity to me more than anything means a great education. . . . [I]t pains me because we do know how to provide a great education. We really do. We could make sure that every young child in this

country got a great education. We fall *far* short of that. . . . I'm
100 percent sure that if it hadn't been for Mrs. Hill in fourth
grade and a few others, I would absolutely have ended up in jail.
I could see those tendencies in myself to have a certain energy
to do something. When you're young, a little bit of course cor-
rection goes a long way.

After high school, he insisted on going to Reed College in Portland,
Oregon; it would mean a difficult strain on the household budget but
his adoptive parents had promised his grad-student birth mother that
they would see the child through college. Their intentions were good
but Steve dropped out after finishing only one semester, though he hung
on to audit classes for some additional months.

He returned to the Valley and got a night job at Atari in order to
save the money to take a "journey to the East." Steve reemerged from
his trip to India as a practicing Zen Buddhist and fruitarian. He went
back to Atari—which was, as far as I can recall, the only job working
for someone else that he has ever had. And he got in touch with Woz,
who had a day job at Hewlett Packard in Palo Alto and in his spare time
was developing printed circuit boards. Woz was a member of the now
legendary Homebrew Computer Club, a collection of young technology
geeks obsessed with computers.

Despite or maybe because of his countercultural background, Steve
has always been particularly astute in seeing business opportunities
others can't see. He saw the work Woz was doing as offering that kind
of opportunity.

Steve had somehow recognized early on that when you want something passionately, you can tap into the power to convince others as
well. Not all that many years before, his family lived in an area served
by a school he didn't want to attend. He announced that he just wouldn't
go there. Still in his early teens, he was able to convince his folks to pull

up stakes and move to a different neighborhood so that he could attend the school he wanted.

At Homebrew, Steve noticed that Woz's buddies were designing circuit-board schematics but not bothering to build what they designed. Steve suggested that Woz build boards and sell them to Homebrew members who weren't getting around to building anything.

Woz couldn't figure out how they could make money doing this. He would later remember, "It wasn't like we both thought it was going to go a long way. It was like, we'll both do it for fun and even though we're gonna lose some money probably. We'll just have been able to say we had a company." Newly inspired, Woz threw in with Steve—the partnership that would become Apple Computer.

In his autobiography, Woz reveals why he really needed the unstoppable Steve. Woz was building what was to become the first Apple computer and he wanted to use DRAM chips from Intel, but they were far too expensive. Steve said he'd handle it. He called Intel and convinced someone in marketing to give him the chips—free. Woz was both dumbfounded and grateful. "I could never have done that. I was way too shy," he says. But for Steve, it was no big deal: A few years earlier, while still in his teens, he had managed to get a phone call through to Hewlett-Packard cofounder William Hewlett, who was intrigued enough to spend nearly half an hour on the phone with him, and reward him with the offer of a summer job.

Passion Isn't Optional: A Lesson in Salesmanship

In 1996, with both NeXT and Pixar still draining money, the happy chance that would save Steve's neck and set him up for all the great things he was to do came from the least likely source, the last place he could possibly have expected.

Apple Computer desperately needed a new operating system. Microsoft Windows, for all its flaws, was appearing in new versions with attractive, convenient new features, drawing away Mac customers. In Steve's absence, Apple seemed to have lost the ability to create a new operating system in-house; a large team of engineers had been laboring for years but was still clearly a long way from a working solution—in part because the man who was supposedly in charge had not been given any real authority.

The company was then in the hands of a skilled PhD technologist, Gil Amelio, who had engineered a remarkable turnaround at chip-maker National Semiconductor and been brought in to Apple to provide technology leadership and solve the financial problems. When it was clear that the Apple engineers were not going to come up with a viable new operating system, Gil began looking outside the walls of One Infinite Loop.

There were soon several formidable candidates for the plum assignment of creating a new Apple OS—notably Microsoft. Bill Gates was making a full court press trying to convince Gil Amelio that Windows NT could be adapted to its long-time rival's needs. Microsoft was a 500-ton gorilla, but the idea of letting the software engineers who had created Windows come up with something just as flawed for Apple was an appalling prospect. And would, besides, have gone over like a lead balloon with the hordes of Macintosh devotees.

As far as Amelio was concerned, having Sun Microsystems develop a version of its SunOS was the leading possibility, but Gil was determined to explore all reasonable alternatives. Another candidate was software called BeOS, developed by ex–Apple executive Jean-Louis Gassée, who several years before was the guy who had been put in charge of the Macintosh team as Steve's replacement. Gil set up technical teams to evaluate each of these prospects, with three of his top software engineers in charge: Wayne Meretsky, Winston Hendrickson, and Kurt Piersol. Each team was tasked to present a written evaluation.

One day in the middle of all this, Gil's chief technology officer, Ellen Hancock, received a call from a NeXT engineer saying that he heard Apple was looking for an operating system. (In fact, Steve may have been pulling the strings behind the scenes. Figuring that a call from him personally would likely not be well received, he may have arranged for that engineer to call.) Ellen told Winston to round up a couple of other engineers and meet with the NeXT engineers and take a look. The team spent time checking out NeXTStep, and Winston reported back that it was a possibility worth considering.

Steve had recognized that NeXT desperately needed some sort of bailout, and a contract to develop the new Apple operating system could just be the answer. And who better to lead that effort than Steve himself.

Meanwhile, Amelio had a setback. The technical evaluations of SunOS had been promising and Gil's negotiations with CEO Scott McNealy had gone well. At the last minute, Sun's board had turned down the deal.

That left NeXT and Be as the final contenders.

The scene was set for a battle royal between Steve and Jean-Louis, especially after Steve read that Gassée had already begun talks with Apple—a news story Gil was convinced had its origins in a calculated leak on Gassée's part.

December 10, 1996, was the date set for the Gunfight at the O.K. Corral. Steve and Jean-Louis were invited to make their case at a showdown session, one after the other, at Palo Alto's Garden Court Hotel, an un-likely meeting location chosen to foil reporters.

Steve came in with his operating system genius, Avie Tevanian, sit-ting at a table placed at the head of an open U-shaped setup, facing Gil and Ellen at the far end. Apple software expert Wayne Meretsky, sitting halfway down along the side table, describes the scene: "Steve's pres-entation was completely directed at Gil, as if there was no one else in the room. Steve was, as one would expect, smooth" as he "extolled the virtues of the OS," ticking off the essential features that made it appropriate for Apple and then demonstrating on a laptop how the NeXTStep operating system could run two movies simultaneously . . . then launched three more—*five* movies running side by side on a single computer. Everyone in the room understood how valuable software that could control so much processing power could be for Apple.

Wayne continues, "Steve pulled out all the stops, and his presentation, in which he tag teamed with Avie, proved once again he is if nothing else the top salesman and orator in the technology business. Gassée turned up by himself without a prepared talk, ready only to entertain questions." He had miscalculated, thinking that Apple had no other realistic choice except his BeOS. He didn't make any sort of real pitch for why BeOS and only BeOS was the solution Apple needed.

As Wayne Meretsky describes it, "The decision to go with NeXT rather than Be Inc. became a no-brainer."

Without revealing Apple's decision, CEO Amelio contacted Steve to see what kind of deal he could make. Again to avoid press leaks, they met at Steve's home. Gil remembers that "Steve is a gifted speaker, and this carries over to his negotiations," but "he promises more than he can deliver in an effort to get you to agree." What was Gil's own negotiating stance? In a variation of the tactic Steve had famously used with John Sculley, Gil says, his approach was, "Do you want to mess around with NeXT or change the world?"

In the end, Apple didn't contract with NeXT for the development of a new Macintosh operating system; instead, Apple purchased Steve's entire company, gaining all rights to NeXTStep, many of NeXT's best talent . . . and Steve Jobs, in the role of consultant to the CEO. People warned Gil that if he allowed Steve back into Apple, Steve would soon take the company away from him. Gil's answer was that he had made the decision that was best for the company.

Only a few months later, Gil Amelio would find himself regretting that he had not insisted on one additional clause in his employment agreement with Apple: that he remain CEO for three years, or even five—long enough that he would have time to complete a turnaround of the company, restoring it to healthy financial condition, with solid products and strong cash flow. He knew bringing the company back to life would take time. He assumed the board would give him the chance to make it all happen.

Of course, he couldn't have foreseen when he was offered the CEO position that Steve Jobs might come to be in a position to take it all away.

No one who knew Steve expected him to do anything less.

The eminent, highly respected *Fortune* business writer Brent Schlender lit the match with a timely article under an incendiary headline: "SOMETHING'S ROTTEN IN CUPERTINO."

The banner title continued in part: "STEVE JOBS HAS RETURNED, WITH A TURNAROUND STRATEGY THAT COULD MAKE APPLE HIS ONCE AGAIN."

You couldn't read the article without gaining a sense that Schlender cared deeply about the fate of Apple, and was convinced that Steve was just the medicine the company needed. He wrote about "a power play . . . in progress that calls into question who's really running the company."

Calling Steve "the Svengali of Silicon Valley," Schlender sounded awed by the terms of the NeXT buyout, with Steve collecting $100 million and 1.5 million shares of Apple stock. And his influence was already being felt: "[H]is fingerprints are all over Amelio's latest reorganization plan and product strategy—even though Jobs doesn't have an operational role or even a board seat."

The capper was Schlender's prediction that Steve might be "scheming" to take over Apple, quoting Steve's best friend, Oracle CEO Larry Ellison, as saying, "Steve's the only one who can save Apple. We've talked about it very seriously many, many times."

Whether or not Steve fed Schlender fodder for the article, he could not have had any better support in his campaign. Steve began secret conversations with board members, focusing in particular on Ed Woolard, chairman of Dupont and a former board member of IBM. Though Woolard had been recruited to the Apple board by Gil, he had become impatient with some of Gil's decisions. It must have weighed heavily on Woolard that Steve had been deemed incapable of running a single operation at Apple—the Macintosh group—and that he had failed to turn NeXT into a viable company. Yet Steve's well-honed power of persuasion came into play once again. Before long Woolard was on the phone, talking to other board members, explaining his thinking, taking a poll. It took some convincing, but within weeks of the Fortune article, two board members, including Mike Markkula, were in favor of letting Gil continue . . . against three others who had come around to side with Woolard. The ax was ready to fall.

Gil was holding a family gathering over the July 4 weekend at his vacation home on the shores of Lake Tahoe when the phone rang. It was Ed Woolard, who said he was calling "with some bad news." He told Gil, "You've done a lot to help the company, but the sales haven't rebounded. We think you need to step down." Gil pointed out that Apple had just reported quarterly results that beat the analyst's predictions, and asked, "You want me to step down just when things are beginning to look better!?"

Woolard replied that the board wanted to "find a CEO who can be a great marketing and sales leader for the company." He didn't mention that they had already agreed on letting Steve run the company as "interim-CEO." Gil hardly needed to be told that Steve would be his replacement: He had been warned.

Steve Jobs was back and he was, for the first time in the history of the company, in full command. *Fortune* editor at large Peter Elkind beautifully described the New Steve, the Takeover/Business Manager Steve: "Right away, Jobs dug into the mucky details of the business, creating a sense of urgency, radically reducing Apple's product line, and accelerating a wholesale cost cutting that would shrink the company back to profitability. Jobs had become a far better leader, less of a go-to-hell aesthete who cared only about making beautiful objects. Now he was a go-to-hell aesthete who cared about making beautiful objects that made money. No engineering spec, no design flourish was too small for his scrutiny."

The observation was only partly correct. For Steve, it's never really been about making money, but the first order of business called for remaking Apple in some painful ways to save it from the dust heap of failed technology companies. He began taking a hard-eyed look at every product and project in the company. According to Senior Engineering Scientist Alex Fielding, "Meetings with Jobs were practically pitch sessions as to why projects should survive." If he didn't like what he heard, or it didn't fit into his vision of only sticking with a few core products, your project was done for, and so was your job.

Alex says, "Gil Amelio had a campaign that said, 'I was there when the comeback began . . .' Ironically, he was right in some ways considering the NeXT merger did bring Jobs back. But many employees now took the 'I was there when the comeback began' bumper stickers and amended them to read, 'I was there when the ~~comeback~~ *layoffs* began.'"

Winston Hendrickson, the software engineer who had originally come back from NeXT with a positive report on the NeXT operating system, was still at Apple. He recalled that in the first half of 1997, there was curiosity as to what it meant for Steve to be a "consultant" to Gil and speculation that the transition of R&D leadership over to former NeXT executives indicated Steve was doing more than just advising. But Steve, Winston says, was "relatively invisible."

At that early stage, Winston remembers, Steve seemed to be "keeping his distance as insurance against the still likely failure of Apple. Many people's antennae were twitching with a feeling that shadowy things were taking place, but the post-acquisition re-organizations and ongoing attrition of talent overshadowed what was happening at the exec level."

As Steve became more visible, it generated a mixture of excitement and trepidation, somewhat typical in any transformation but at the same time, Winston remembers, also unique with an uncomfortable air of "what's next?" Decisions and changes were finally happening—and at an unprecedented pace for Apple of that era. This generated a high level of excitement, in part from the fact that "the scale and velocity of the actions made it progressively more clear there was a new sheriff in town."

Gil's departure brought the same mixed reaction, leaving "no doubt whatsoever that NeXT had really bought Apple" rather than the other way around. Curiously, Winston thinks, Apple employees—or at least the engineers—"were thirsty for leadership" and even for "the specter of an autocrat who had long been yearned for over the years of inde-cisiveness that marked the early '90s."

Soon after he became interim-CEO, Steve jumped on the hardware teams and "drove significant cuts—from hundreds of projects down to double digits." At a top-100 managers offsite in Pajaro Dunes, Steve himself pitched the hardware plans, unveiling the project that would become the iMac. Winston had the chance to speak with Steve one-on-one during the dinner reception and "felt that I was being sized up."

But he had learned from observing the NeXT people that you could disagree with Steve if you were thoughtful and reasoned, and he found that to be true: "I disagreed with one of his justifications for the iMac and was only told I was wrong and why, rather than being 'roasted' as most people assumed would be the case." (Winston discovered in time that his call was wrong, and that Steve, the non-engineer, had it right.)

Steve once told me one of his goals for Apple was to be a billion-dollar company with fewer than 5,000 employees. He said he had set this goal because it would rank Apple as the—or at least one of the—most lucrative and productive companies in the United States. It's no surprise that he didn't manage to hold the number of employees in check—the retail stores alone now account for some 1,500—but he certainly overshot his market-capitalization goal. The company's market cap, as of this writing, is more than $280 billion.

The CEO and the Board of Directors

One thing that Steve learned from the whole wrenching experience of being exiled was the importance of a board of directors that understands what the head of the company is doing strategically. In retrospect, he might have seen the writing on the wall when the Apple board gave the "1984" ad a cold reception.

Everyone knows that a "good board of directors" is critical to a successful company. But what does a "good board" really mean? More than anything, it means board members who understand the company, its vision, and its CEO. Even if the CEO hasn't been instrumental in selecting the members, he or she should know the background and qualifications of each member, what role each plays, and who does and doesn't subscribe to the company vision.

The ideal board is a group of people with differing business experiences who use the company's product religiously and have a very clear understanding of who the customer is and where the business should be in five years.

Did you notice I didn't mention profit? Profit is an outcome of the product and the people who run the company. As I've said before, it's the product that is a company's heart.

When Steve gained the reins at Apple, he remade the board, giving the boot to all but two members. One he retained, of course, was Ed Woolard, who had played such a key role in Steve's return. The other was Gareth Chang, a senior VP of Hughes Electronics. He added close friend Larry Ellison, and former Apple exec Bill Campbell (sometimes called "Coach" because—unlikely as this sounds—he had at one time been the football coach at Columbia University). Steve's motives were clear: This was no board of "yes men," but they were people who thought like Steve, trusted him, and would support his efforts to rescue and rebuild the company.

I learned about boards the hard way. In one of my start-up companies, in order to get funded, I had to accept executives and board members handpicked by Lehman Brothers. These folks had all the qualifications but were only focused on the numbers. If someone had told me they didn't even know what the product was, it wouldn't have surprised me. None even used the product, a telltale sign that they didn't understand the company's vision or direction.

But Steve, with his new board, had brought with him a new conviction, one that most companies can't afford to ignore: A company can stay true to its core business while still making more than one kind of product. That's where he was now headed.

Holistic Product Development

It's said that Christopher Columbus was able to find in one town people with all the different skills needed for building and equipping his ships—carpenters, sail makers, rope makers, craftsmen to make the caulking, and the rest, as well as the sailors themselves.

Today, most products of any complexity—and a lot of very simple ones as well—include components or ingredients not created on-site but purchased elsewhere, from some other company.

It's the reason Android cell phones don't work as well as the iPhone: because Google makes the Android software, which then runs on hardware from a number of different manufacturers. The cell phone manufacturers don't control the design of the software, and Google doesn't have any way of making sure that the hardware designs will be compatible with the Droid software. (I'll come back to this idea a bit later.)

It's why the rim at the top of the can of Gillette shaving cream always turns rusty: Gillette makes the shaving cream but buys the cans from a supplier—a nameless manufacturing company that doesn't have to take any flak from Gillette customers. (And one wonders whether Gillette's top managers aren't using their own product; if they were, wouldn't they have corrected the problem a long time ago?)

By the time of his return to Apple, Steve had begun to understand what he would come to consider a fundamental, essential question: How is it possible to produce a product that works well if the group creating the software and the group creating the hardware work entirely independently of each other?

His answer: It's *not* possible.

But if you think that question only applies to companies in high-tech, you're in for a surprise. We are rapidly reaching a time when many mundane, everyday products will have a computer chip in them, and these products will communicate with one another in ways we're only just beginning to conceive.

Many home washing machines have been controlled by computer chips for years. And have you noticed how a Prius or Lexus owner unlocks his car and starts it? Not with a key but with a "keyless" gadget containing a computer chip. Electronics in the car recognize a signal being emitted by the gadget and unlock the car as the driver approaches, then allow him to start the car just by pressing the ignition button.

That's a foretaste of the future.

So don't send to know for whom this chapter is about: It's likely about tomorrow's version of your own products.

I've come to call this marriage of software and hardware the "Holistic Product Development" concept; it has become an essential part of Steve's product philosophy, and of mine. And even if you're not in high-tech, it will need to become part of yours sooner than you imagine.

(I'm not sure how Steve came by the term "holistic," but I just became aware one day that he was using it to describe the complete product development process.)

Embracing the New

Steve Jobs believes that you cannot design a product with focus groups, not when you're trying to be truly original. He loved to quote Henry Ford, who once said something like, "If I had asked my customers what they wanted, they would have told me, 'A faster horse.'"

Every time I heard Steve bring up that quote, it made me think of that 1932 Model A Ford I got as a reward for my work on the ranch. Even as a fifteen year-old, I was able to do all the repairs on the car without an owner's manual; it was all straightforward. If you had enough basic knowledge, and a fair amount of common sense, that was all you needed. The Model A was a well-designed product. And Ford's using the crates that the parts were delivered in as structure elements for the seats and flooring offers another example of holistic product development. If Steve Jobs and Henry Ford had met, I'm certain they would have found a lot in common and parted with great admiration for each other.

Ford's comment about the horse carries an implication that Steve grasps intuitively. If you ask a group of people, even people who aren't dissatisfied with a product, how to make it better, the odds are that they'll spend most of their time trying to think of things that are wrong with it. That fault-finding has some value. But the best you'll get is some guidance about how to make incremental improvements. It won't give you ideas for dramatically new products that are game changers. It's not innovation.

Why not? Because in a situation like that, most people concentrate on what they think they have been assigned to think about. They think they've been assigned to focus on what their experience has been. That's the wrong focus.

What you need are people who focus on what their experience *could be*.

The thing that separates visionaries from most of humanity is their tendency to wonder about what they could do or how different their lives or their products could be. If you give such people new tools or new technologies, they immediately begin to wonder about creating products that will enable them to do completely new things.

Innovators create products that are an outgrowth of what they imagine, things that help them create a world they would like to live in. That's a drastically different mind-set from just figuring out how to improve upon the past.

Brilliant product developers are driven by a desire for change, for things and experiences that are different, better, and special. Product developers like Steve Jobs have imagination that enables them to envision those new products or new ways of living. Then they ask *Why not?* This always reminds me of Robert Kennedy's line, "Some people see things as they are and ask, 'Why?' I dream things that never were and ask, 'Why not?'"

People with Kennedy's outlook, on discovering that creating a dramatically different product has become possible, will ask, "Why wait?"

Why not? Why wait?

Thoreau said, "Simplification of means and elevation of ends is the goal." Well, the product development version of that view is to conceive of something completely different and better, and then figure out how to make it.

I've often heard Steve explain why Apple's products look so good or work so well by telling the "show car" anecdote. "You see a show car," he would say (I'm paraphrasing here, but this is pretty close to his words), "and you think, 'That's a great design, it's got great lines.' Four or five years later, the car is in the showroom and in television ads, and it sucks. And you wonder what happened. They had it. They had it, and then they lost it."

And then Steve would offer his version of what went wrong: "When the designers took that great idea to the engineers, the engineers said, 'No way—we can't do that. It's impossible.' They were allowed to go off and do what they figured was 'possible,' and then they turned their plans over to the people in manufacturing. The manufacturing people said, 'We can't build that.'" He loved to finish by saying, "They had grabbed defeat from the jaws of victory."

Steve would probably say that the problem is not feasibility. It's that the car company did not make an unconditional commitment to create the best product, to make something really new and different, even when they could imagine it.

To be a holistic product developer, you have to do more than imagine something new; you also have to embrace novelty, commit to it. You have to feel that making something different, better, and special is *the* most important thing.

In so many firms there are imaginative people whose brilliant ideas are frequently discarded in favor of sustaining the status quo. In a society that customarily applauds innovation, a multitude of great ideas are getting thwarted and squandered every day. That's why you read so often about cases where an entrepreneur with a brilliant new product leaves his previous company because they had no interest in his visionary ideas.

There were times when that almost happened at Apple. In 1997, when Steve came back to the company, he and Jonathan Ive, the head of design, developed the prototype of the iMac. It was a computer integrated with a flamboyant, neon-colored cathode-ray display. It looked like something from a sci-fi cartoon as drawn by a precocious, imaginative child.

Steve later told *Time*'s Lev Grossman, "Sure enough . . . when we took it to the engineers, they came up with 38 reasons [why it couldn't be done]. And I said, 'No, no, we're doing this.' And they said, 'Well, Why?' And I said, 'Because I'm the CEO and I think it can be done.' And so they kind of begrudgingly did it. But then it was a big hit."

In this case the show car got built.

Partnering

The sources of Steve's creative instincts were sometimes more than a little surprising. As unlikely as it may sound, he was a huge fan of Gutenberg, over and over bringing up in our conversations his fascination with the way Gutenberg's press operated and the impact that this one invention had on all of human society.

One day it suddenly hit him: The Macintosh wouldn't just display and print letters and numbers like other computers, it would create graphics, too. Users could create company logos, advertising flyers, and all kinds of things dressed up with artwork, so obviously the Mac deserved a companion printer that would be able to print in ways that went beyond what a dot-matrix printer could do.

Steve said, "We need something like what Gutenberg did."

I thought, "Oh, sure—how likely is that!" On the other hand, where there's a Steve, there's a way.

He talked to Bob Belleville about the problem. Both knew there wasn't time to invent a suitable printer, not one that would be ready for sale any time soon after the Mac was launched.

Belleville had what seemed like a brilliant suggestion. On a trip to Japan, he had visited Canon and been shown their laser copiers. It might be possible, he said, to take a laser copier and adapt it so it could print from the Mac. If that was right, they could put together an engineering team to create a card that would interface between the two—

translating data from the Mac into whatever form was needed by the printer.

Steve was beginning to imagine it already. He said, "Let's go see them."

Calls were made to Canon, arrangements set up, and the entire first-class section of an Air Japan flight was booked. Six of us would be going: Steve and Bob, three engineers, and me.

On the flight, the engineers built a mock-up out of cardboard representing the maximum size adapter card we could use that would fit into the available space within the Canon printer.

When we arrived in Tokyo, as we entered the hotel, some young girls recognized Steve and rushed up for autographs. I was blown away: Steve was a familiar face on the major news magazines in the United States but nobody ever asked for his autograph. Here we were half a world away, and Steve was not only recognized but giggled over as if he were a rock star. I wasn't sure how he would react, and watched closely; if he was annoyed, finding this an intrusion on his rather strong sense of privacy, he didn't show it. In fact, though I knew he'd never admit it (and I knew he wouldn't like it if I asked), I got the distinct feeling that he was secretly pleased.

When I got to my room, I was in for a surprise. Asked in advance what type of room I wanted, and being what I think of as the kind of traveler who's always interested in the local culture, I chose "Traditional Japanese." My room had no bed, just a mat on the floor. I toughed it out, though it sure wasn't the best night's sleep I ever had.

Cultural Differences

The next morning the gang of us was picked up by limo and driven to the Canon headquarters in Tokyo, arriving at ten. In a conference room, we were treated to tea, coffee, and pastries. Everyone was being very deferential to Steve, again treating him like a rock star, though in a different sense than the girls the night before had.

Then the Canon chairman and CEO joined, with introductions that were ceremonial and quite formal. Once the chairman had left, we settled down with the CEO and half a dozen others to begin the business discussion, Steve explaining what we wanted to do, a little impatient at having to wait for the translator after each sentence or two.

But there turned out to be a bigger cultural problem than the translating. The Japanese weren't responding; in fact, it looked almost as if they had gone to sleep—sitting with heads bowed and eyes closed. Steve was beginning to get frustrated, shooting me glances of annoyance. We had come all this way and he was putting them to sleep?!

Fortunately, on the way over I had read a pamphlet prepared by Air Japan for foreigners, which explained that in a business meeting, the Japanese will sometimes close their eyes to avoid being distracted by the visual, listening for the pure essence of words. I whispered this to him. He gave me a quick small smile of understanding and appreciation, and dived back in.

Lunchtime showed the Canon people had gone out of their way to please Steve. They had found out what he liked to eat and treated us to a lavish meal at a leading sushi restaurant. Protocol apparently called for business to be set aside over lunch in favor of personal conversation. Steve wanted to talk about business all the way through, and did.

The afternoon conversations with the Canon president, head of development, and attorney, hit on some sticking points. For one thing, they didn't like being told that the Apple technology was proprietary, so we would not be shipping our chips to them for installation in the printers. Instead, they would ship the innards of the machines to the U.S., where the Apple chips would be installed at an Apple plant, and the whole works then dropped into Apple-designed cases.

The president had problems with this but after some Stevian persuasion gave in and agreed.

Next came the discussion that Steve had correctly anticipated was going to be the big issue of the visit: The case would bear an Apple logo; the Canon name would not appear. Steve was right—this turned into a *huge* discussion issue. He went back and forth with the Canon people for what was probably a full hour.

The reason this was such a big deal for Canon was that they considered the association with Apple Computer, a company so admired and respected in Japan, to be something that would bring them honor, increasing their reputation and sales. Steve made concessions: They could run ads saying Canon built the engine driving the Apple laser printer; they could have their name on their drive engine inside the printer. But he was unmovable about the basic issue, and used his full persuasive powers.

One of the Canon people—I don't recall if it was the president or the head of development—raised another issue. They wanted Steve to develop a way that the Mac could display Kanji characters, which would make the Macintosh usable throughout Japan. (Kanji are Chinese characters widely used in the modern Japanese writing system.) Steve turned to Bob Belleville, who said he'd have to talk to his engineers in Cupertino.

The meeting adjourned for the phone call. Meanwhile I was put together with Canon's equivalent of a Human Resources boss, who had lots of questions for me about how we compensated our workers, how we motivated them, how we decided on promotions, and so on. I don't imagine Canon ever adopted any of our practices but I was fascinated that they wanted to know.

When the big meeting resumed, Bob announced that he and his engineers agreed they could indeed give the Macintosh the capability of displaying and using Kanji.

Finally the Canon president said they would agree to Steve's condition that no Canon name appear on the case of the printer. Steve, Bob, and I all understood: This decision was not made because he had decided it was the right thing to do; it had been made only because he had so much respect for Steve Jobs and Apple Computer.

I'm convinced that Steve learned a lesson from this experience. It changed his thinking. This was the first time Mac had gone fishing for a development partner outside the company, and it made the Laser-Writer possible far earlier than if Steve had set software and hardware teams to work on the project, to develop Apple's own laser printer from scratch.

From then on, Steve would always be open to looking for outside solutions, especially for the first generation of a groundbreaking product. And though he had at that time not yet come to his understanding about holistic product development, he was already following the principle of the concept. This experience plus the Twiggy lesson were two major factors in changing his thinking.

On this trip, we also visited Sony, in Kyoto. Talk about a mutual admiration society. The Sony Walkman was one of the products Steve loved. He could talk endlessly about the simplicity of design and function. It was a favorite topic in meetings with the Mac engineers. He often spoke about Sony as "the Apple of Japan" and his model for producing incredibly original products. The visit to Sony was like a trip to Mecca for him.

Where the Canon buildings were in the traditional Japanese style that we saw everywhere, the architecture of the Sony buildings would make them look appropriate in Los Angeles, Chicago, or Manhattan. Once we walked inside, though, we found them quite austere, by American standards rather cold in design.

The one big exception was the office of the CEO, Akio Morita. As we walked in, we couldn't help noticing the original Van Gogh hanging on his wall. I found him to be very Westernized, very intelligent, artic-ulate, entrepreneurial, and sophisticated. Morita-san spoke good English, as did all of his top executives. I'd learned later that he came from an old, established family that had been in the business of brewing sake, the Japanese rice wine, for some four hundred years.

The Sony execs, like those at Canon, were clearly huge fans of Steve, treating him with reverence—almost as if he were a head of state. That evening, they took us to the most extraordinary dinner I've ever had. It was the six of us, escorted by Morita-san and five of his top people. Bob Belleville was a great companion on these occasions, both for his tech-nological savvy and for his knack for socializing; culturally sophisticated and with good insight, he gently tutored Steve in the right conduct, from professional etiquette to dinner traditions, and Steve listened.

The Sony dinner was at a restaurant so exclusive that it has only a single table, and dining there is a privilege handed down from generation to generation . . . but with one hitch: There is no guarantee that when the father dies, the son will be accepted.

The dishes that evening included blowfish. As you probably know, unless it's prepared with very great care by someone who knows exactly what he's doing, blowfish is deadly—considered the second-most deadly vertebrate in the world. We all figured that if our Japanese hosts trusted the chef enough to eat it, we should be unafraid, as well. And I suppose it would have been an insult for one of us to say he didn't dare, showing a lack of trust. In case you've ever wondered, blowfish turned out to be very white and something like cod but—to me, at least—without much taste. Steve, though, told our hosts not only how much he liked it but that he hoped to find it served in the United States so he could try it again. (In the right kind of restaurant, I'd try it again myself—but only to see whether I'd like the taste better the second time.)

I came away from our Sony day with a sense that despite the differ-ence in cultures and the—what?—perhaps fifty years difference in age,

Steve and Morita held amazingly similar values. At bottom, you knew Morita-san was calling for the creation of products he himself wanted, just like Steve. And both of them had made their companies leading examples of practicing holistic product development.

It was like a transcultural confirmation of everything Steve stood for: Love what you do. Love what you make. Make it to perfection.

And listening to the two of them talk was like a lesson in business values for everybody else. In the end, the sad part is that the Apple-Sony relationship never reached its potential: Steve would too soon be leaving Apple, and by the time he returned, Morita-san would have left Sony.

Quality over Quantity

Everyone applauds innovation and innovators because we all believe that great products lead to great profits. In addition, we just love to be amazed and delighted by something that's a breakthrough and so cool that it expands our concept of the world and what we will be able to do that we couldn't do before. We're all addicted to novelty. In that sense we're all early adopters.

But for people who create the products, the desire gets cranked up much earlier: They have to develop the products in order to play with them or enjoy them.

It's not enough to think of a terrific product and want to make it. It's being able to do it. Where does that ability come from?

In Steve's case, of course in large part the ability derives from his focus and his undeviating commitment to his strategy. But Steve is also a businessman. In part Apple's innovations result from his intuitive grasp of the trade-offs required and his willingness to make those trade-offs. He has been willing to accept amazing risks to realize his vision. He is willing to pay the price that's required of anyone determined to commit to innovation.

Recall that one of the first things Steve did on becoming interim-CEO was to stop selling dozens of products. It's one thing to sketch a cool product on the back of a napkin or BS about it at a meeting of eager designers who are sort of your disciples. But what about those legacy products that are steady sellers?

They may not be iPods or iPhones, yet even the most lackluster Apple merchandise was bringing in revenues and earnings. They were paying for themselves and helping to keep Apple solvent. Every one of those dull items was connecting Apple to a reliable stream of revenues, even if, in some cases, it was a tributary or just a trickle. It's a scary move to pull the plug on those established, steady-selling workhorses of your product line.

But as we've seen, that's what Steve did. He cut dozens of products and devoted resources to just four. That came as a surprise even to the board. Apple's chairman at the time was Edgar Woolard, CEO of DuPont, who said, "Our jaws dropped when we heard that one." Industry commentators and Wall Street analysts have often pressed Steve to grow Apple's market share by selling products that were commodities or by moving into segments in which the company would not be the leader. Steve has never buckled under to such pressure.

"I'm as proud of what we don't do as I am of what we do," he has often said.

There are different ways to interpret that quote. But I've always thought he meant we show our values and our vision also by what we choose not to do. We're not trying to be all things to all people, even though trying to please everyone is sometimes tough to resist and can seem like the way to get rich. "Quality is more important than quantity, and it's a better financial decision," Steve told *BusinessWeek*. "One home run is much better than two doubles."

What enables Steve to focus is, I think, the ability to envision the future and his driving need to make it happen. And there's one other factor, as well: competition, or simply the belief in having the better mousetrap. Steve from early on has seen each new great product as holding the potential of drawing more people to turn away from Windows computers and become Mac users.

I think the Steve Jobs I came to know all those years ago won't be satisfied until at least half of all computer sales are Macintoshes.

Building the Holistic Company

To have true innovation, you have to build a culture to support it. *Innovation*, with a capital *I*, is one of the most overused words in business, because having innovative products is code for saying that in some sense you are outdoing the competition. A lot of companies "message" by using the word *innovation* without really doing it or being it. It's nothing but marketing spin or a halfhearted, transparent attempt to motivate the troops.

To be an entrepreneurial company, new ideas must become the lifeblood of the organization. How can you foster new ideas in a traditional corporate culture?

You can't. It doesn't work. Entrepreneurial companies and traditional companies are two fundamentally different organisms. You can't get innovation from a traditional company. Most of the time, at ordinary conventional companies, an employee takes his or her idea to a more senior manager, who may take credit for the idea and in some cases even get promoted for it. Customarily the more senior manager gets to manage the project and the person who thought of the idea gets a pat on the back but nothing more. This is the pernicious behavior pattern of traditional companies that operate in a hierarchical fashion. Not that they don't produce good ideas. Good ideas happen wherever you have thinking people, which is everywhere. But at traditional companies those ideas too often get thwarted, trashed, imperfectly developed, or misappropriated.

By contrast, in an entrepreneurial environment, receptiveness and reward for new ideas are the ways to engage people to give their best and feel they have a stake in the company. Through ideas, people challenge one another in a way that is not invidious. You inspire competition and aspiration by showing your belief that each person can express creativity in his or her own way. This may be in accounting, product design, or a new way to provide incentives for employees.

But there's a "gotta": You've gotta have a vision for people to follow—a road map into infinity. You encourage ideas that are aligned with the vision and road map, and then give people a chance to be a part of it.

You also have to tolerate mistakes without penalizing people. Believe me, it makes a big impression when someone who originated an idea that the company adopted and put funding into gets demoted or even gets fired when the project doesn't pan out.

When the opposite is the case, everyone gets the message: It's okay to be creative, to do something new—your job isn't going to be at stake.

Through encouraging employees and their ideas, you get a grassroots intelligence network. Employees will bring in new things in the market to talk about them, discuss their advantages and shortcomings, test them, play with them . . . and then wonder, "What can we do that's a generation better?"

In traditional companies, people are so focused on productivity and profits that they don't have time to look at things from a radically different perspective. At least not the majority of employees in most companies. And there isn't much cross-pollination, because too many companies keep a playpen for really bright people, off in some separate lab or area where they can't mess up the business side of things. They segregate the oddball geniuses and limit their influence for innovation. This practice is organized in a way that frustrates or limits creativity instead of encouraging it throughout the organization.

Maybe I'm just a dreamer, but I believe the entrepreneurial organization represents the future because people are demanding this type of environment. I've seen it in my own companies and I've seen it elsewhere. People want more humane environments where their efforts are at least acknowledged, where they feel a part of something. The youngest generation of employees, and especially the most talented ones, want more than a nine-to-five job. They want something with purpose.

Some Innovation Lessons

The earlier iMac story offers three lessons about how innovation happens—one about collaboration, one about control, and one about inspiring employees.

Apple employees talk all the time about "deep collaboration," "cross-pollination," or "concurrent engineering." What they mean is that there aren't discrete, linear, sequential development stages. Instead, it's simultaneous and holistic. Products get worked on in parallel by all departments—design, hardware, and software—at the same time in endless rounds of interdisciplinary design reviews. Products don't pass from team to team. Everyone who has made an investment stays invested. No one is made to walk away from their involvement.

Managers elsewhere boast about how little time they waste in meetings. Apple is big on them and proud of it. "The conventional way of developing products just doesn't work when you're as ambitious as we are," says designer extraordinaire Jonathan Ive. "When the challenges are that complex, you have to develop a product in a more collaborative, integrated way."

The second lesson from this example is about control. While it's clear that Steve pulled rank and insisted that the iMac would get made, to focus on that would be to overlook how his determination cleared the decks for innovation. Nothing in companies is as blinding as a strategy, an approach, or a product line that has worked before. Success can be self-defeating, if it leads you into the rut of repeating yourself. Too often we cannot envision a different world because we've gotten into the habit of looking at our world with the mind-set of what has worked before.

When Steve committed Apple to the new iMac prototype, he was insisting that the company be open-minded, experimental, and willing to try new things. Doing things differently or making different things, rather than just iterations of "same old, same old" is often what makes a compelling vision appear and lure us. That's what the new can do. It can yank us into a world where the horizon leads somewhere we're excited to go, where creativity happens. When Steve insisted that Apple create this wild-ass, playful looking computer, he was obliterating regimentation.

Even more important, by committing the company to this new iMac, he was offering, implicitly, an amazing and empowering incentive to all of Apple. He was saying that, at Apple, what you can imagine can get made. Good employees find that incredibly inspiring.

That's the third lesson.

Of course, you have to do all the other, time-honored things that engage and gratify employees. You have to be accessible to them, you have to get to know them and learn what motivates them. You have to listen. And you have to appreciate their ideas, even those that are about, say, packaging or documentation. (Small details like product packaging or user manuals can have a big impact on the success of a product. How many times have you bought something and found the owner's manual so complicated that you spent hours learning to assemble the product or use it?)

But the key ingredient, if you've hired the right sort of employees in the first place, is to create a culture where their ideas will have a high probability of being realized. One of the most radioactive isotopes in Steve's powerful charisma is the fact that he has convinced his workers he will commit to innovations. That's what elicits innovation and creates a culture of innovation.

"Apple is an incredibly collaborative company," Steve said at the 2010 All Things Digital conference. "You know how many committees we have at Apple? Zero. We're structured like a start-up. We're the biggest start-up on the planet. What I do all day is meet with teams of people and work on ideas and new problems to come up with new products."

By contrast, some companies are the equivalent of an innovation landfill. They are garbage dumps where great ideas go to die. At PARC, the key development people kept leaving because they never saw their products get into the market. They wanted to see the innovative product they conceived, their pride and joy, end up in the hands of users. And it didn't happen. That's why PARC had its high turnover rate.

I love the way journalist Lev Grossman described it in *Time Magazine*: "If you smooshed together Microsoft, Dell, and Sony into one company, you would have something like the diversity of the Apple technological biosphere."

Evangelizing
Innovation

In Steve Jobs's world, products are not created by one or two or three product idea–people supported by a flock of hands-on engineers or artisans who turn the ideas into working products. That's not the Steve Jobs way and it never has been.

This isn't something he thought on for a while and finally had a bright idea about. He works from the gut, intuitively, and knew from the first that if he assembled the right team, they would together provide enough creative horsepower to turn his dreams into real-life products.

In Steve's world, innovation is a group activity. This was all the more remarkable to me because, as I said, at IBM I had seen the dark side, the depressing side, of innovation. Big Blue had some of the most creative scientists and engineers in the world—entire labs, one after another, filled with these enormously gifted people, an almost unbelievable collection of world-class talent. I found it mind-boggling. So why did I also find it depressing?

Right: All these amazingly inventive people were coming up with phenomenal ideas for new products and improvements to existing products, hardly any of which would ever see the light of day.

Of course, IBM wasn't alone in this deaf-and-dumb world. Kodak, the leader in photography products, kept on doing what they knew so well how to do . . . and completely missed the age of digital picture-taking and digital image processing. If left up to Kodak, after a family holiday or a child's graduation, we'd still be dropping off rolls of film at the drugstore.

Steve understood without having to think about it that innovation is not only a team sport, it needs to be evangelized—both internally and, as well, for outside partners. When you have opened up innovation to outside resources, they need to operate as part of your team. The Mac group practiced this in the early days, when a team of "evangelists" was out beating the drum with developers to create applications.

The Whole-Product Theory

From day one, Steve has lived a philosophy that is an extension of the holistic product development concept. This one says that you cannot produce successful technology products—products that work well and live up to expectations—unless the company that created the hardware also creates the software. I came to call his stance on this "the Whole-Product Theory."

For a time I argued with Steve about the notion. I thought that if we sold our software, as Microsoft does, we could have a better product and control the software market.

He convinced me I was wrong, and he did that not just with his reasoned explanations but, over time, by my witnessing the success of Apple's products and the deficiencies of just about everybody else's. In order to get the best performance of the software running on the hardware, you need to control the total system. The principle isn't just for technology companies: If Steve made mattresses, he wouldn't just design the frame and then buy the springs from the lowest bidder.

If Microsoft had controlled the hardware, they would have produced a much better product than the Windows software we know. Since they don't delve into the problems of developing computer hardware, they simply can't understand what's needed to make software and hardware work well together. Each version of the Windows operating system has had annoying, nagging problems.

The company has done even worse with their consumer products. They have made one product after another that has failed miserably. In mid-2010, they withdrew their new cell phone, the Kin, from the market, after about two months. As one reporter quipped, there will be no next of Kin. But then before you could turn around, the folks from Redmond were back for another try, this one completely different. Dubbed the Windows Phone 7, it quickly drew an unflattering reaction from the *New York Times* in an article headlined, "A Phone of Promise, With Flaws." The article complained that even the name was misleading. "It's not Windows. It doesn't look or work like Windows, doesn't run Windows software, doesn't even require a Windows PC." And while it "shows some real genius, it is missing an embarrassingly long list of features that are standard on iPhone and Android."

Most developers writing software to go into other companies' products take a businesslike approach to the arrangement, aiming to make the best deal for their own company, not the best products for the consumer.

Imagine this scenario: You are the head of product development at Motorola and you've scheduled meetings with Microsoft to discuss your Droid product road map for building Windows Mobile wireless handsets. The meeting goes well. The presentations are professional and end with Microsoft talking about "getting really aggressive in license fees" for

Windows Mobile. They are willing to give up to a 20 percent discount on the license fee per unit.

Following the meeting with Microsoft, you meet with Google to discuss plans for using their Android operating system for your cell phones. Here again, their presentation goes well and is very professional. Both firms have excellent software developers.

But a strange thing happens when the Android folks discuss business terms. They explain that they don't charge any license fee since they are an open-source environment. Rather, they are willing to have you produce Android handsets at no charge. Free is a pretty good deal. Now, to be sure, if Android wasn't any good, free would be meaningless, but if the software turns out to be rock-solid, free will be a very good deal indeed.

Droid users tend to be frustrated by the constant annoying problems that plague their phones. I know a pair of twin brothers who each bought the Motorola Droid. Between them they have had *eight* phones. Motorola keeps replacing the units because they are not working properly. None of the steps, such as returning the phone to the factory-default state, corrected the problems. And who's at fault—Motorola or Google? The consumer doesn't know whom to blame.

iPhone users may get frustrated by dropped calls, but that's mainly the fault of spotty AT&T service. Droid-type problems, in which the device doesn't function as it should, are rare. Yes, there was an issue with the antenna of the iPhone 4 when it was introduced. I put it down to a couple of things. Steve, because of his health, was spending more time with family and yielding some authority to trusted lieutenants for the extraordinary level of attention to detail he always carried on his own shoulders in the past.

Secondly, when you are touted as number one in all business aspects, you need to act like number one. The media has high expectations of direct communications. Apple was not as forthcoming with an immediate response and accepting responsibility as everyone expected, and the media jumped all over the company for the initial period of silence. An inside source tells me that as soon as news of the antenna problem started appearing in the media and on the web, the vice president in charge of the iPhone received a phone call from Steve with a brief message: "That's not the way we do things at Apple." As I understand it, that VP was out of a job: He's no longer working at Apple.

Going Out of House

At Apple, the phrase "Whole Product" means way more than the device. It means the entire experience of using the device. The goal is to design the product so it fits into the natural ways of life, how people customarily use things, rather than expect people to adapt—aiming to create a satisfying sense of the natural, intuitive, and simple.

By 2000, Apple faced a challenge with the whole-product approach. No company can do everything, especially when faced with serious financial restraints, and one page of Apple's ledger continued to look pathetic. The Macintosh still held less than a 3 percent share of the computer market. Steve was desperate for gotta-have applications that might draw Windows users to switch over to the Mac.

It was natural that music-lover Steve would come upon the idea of offering a superior music software package for keeping track of your tunes and letting you quickly locate and play whatever you were looking for.

Ever since the LaserWriter deal with Canon, Steve had been convinced that there are times to develop in-house, and there are times to look around and see what's already out there.

A leading MP3 music software product then on the market was SoundJam MP, developed by Casady and Greene (C&G), a small Silicon Valley firm that had also created a number of Macintosh games.

SoundJam's main programmer, Jeff Robbin, had worked at Apple at one time. SoundJam MP became a big success, garnering 90 percent of the market.

Apple approached C&G about buying SoundJam rights. As part of the deal, Jeff Robbin was hired back by Apple and put in charge of creating a new interface. When the Apple version of the software was introduced at Macworld in January 2001, now renamed "iTunes," it proved immensely popular . . . yet few could have imagined the revolution in consumer habits that it would lead to. Or rather, few other than Steve Jobs and his iTunes team.

At the time, iTunes looked like a stand-alone product. Now we recognize it as the first installment in Steve's overall product strategy.

Product Decisions

Steve had been keeping in touch with work being done at Carnegie Mellon University on advanced software known as the Mach kernel; a kernel is the core segment of an operating system, and Steve had learned enough about the Carnegie Mellon work to believe that this package was likely the best software available to become the basis of a new generation operating system for personal computers; before leaving Apple, he had ordered a Cray supercomputer to start development work for a Mach-kernel-based OS. (That had caused some friction: Steve had spending authority up to a maximum of $10 million, and the Cray cost about $12 million.)

He didn't get to work with the Mach kernel at Apple, but the door was open for making it the basis of the operating system he would need for the new computer he would build at NeXT. He sought out one of the leaders of the Mach kernel work at Carnegie Mellon, Avadis Tevanian, Jr. Avie held an undergraduate degree in math and a masters, and PhD in computer science, and was one of the main developers of the Mach kernel from back in his undergraduate days. Avie said that, yes, he would move to Silicon Valley and go to work for Apple.

Avie had the smarts, the experience, the drive, and the enthusiasm for what Steve was setting out to do. It proved to be a good decision for them both. Avie would become the brains behind creating the NeXTStep operating system software (based of course on the Mach kernel); that software would prove to be a Hail Mary pass for NeXT and for Steve. Avie would later follow Steve to Apple, where he would head up the creation of a new generation of the Macintosh operating system, OS X ("OS-ten"). At the time, no one—not even Steve or Avie—could have imagined that a pared-down version of OS X would make possible the development of the world's most user-friendly, most advanced cell phone.

In any year, Steve's engineers and product team–leaders consider hundreds of ideas, among them more than a few that seem brilliant. But for the moment, I'd like to look at the origins that led to Steve's decision about one particular idea, that led to, "We're going to go with this one."

By always keeping close tabs on the cutting edge of technology, Apple teams are ready to pounce when all of the elements to make some particular new product possible become available. It was a natural once iTunes was pumping that Steve, and Ruby and his teams, would start thinking about a player, an MP3-type device that would be as sexy and groundbreaking as the original Macintosh. But the needed pieces just weren't there.

We've already seen how Steve, after he became interim-CEO, canceled many of the Apple products. Among those that got ash-canned was the company's groundbreaking PDA, the Newton, which Steve dumped because he recognized it wasn't a core product.

Yet a few years later, when Apple was in a more solid position financially, the picture had changed. The market for PDAs was growing briskly. Sales of portable music players were limping; PDAs appeared like a better opportunity than music players. But long before the smart-phone market took off, Steve sensed that cell phones would be able to do things that people were using their PDAs for. Increasingly he came to expect that the PDA market would erode. He turned his back on the PDA and instead cast his gaze elsewhere.

Steve and Jon Rubinstein, looking around for the next product, saw creative designs happening with digital still and video cameras, with music players, and with cell phones. Just to see where it might lead, Ruby set teams to work evaluating the hardware and software various companies were using for all those devices. He learned that the cameras had decent enough software, but for the digital music players, "What was out there was awful," Ruby told *Cornell Engineering Magazine*. "They were big and they were heavy. The user interfaces were terrible."

Meanwhile, Steve was gripped by a sense of the magnitude of the music player market. Even better, the market was appealing because the competition wasn't very threatening and looked like a market ripe for dominating with a product that would revolutionize the user experience.

Sometimes most everything looks right for an idea to turn into an active development project, except that there are some technology gaps, one or two crucial items that don't meet the Apple standards. But this time, the stars were aligned.

Visiting Toshiba in Japan not long before, Ruby was discussing the hard drives the company was providing for various Apple products when a passing mention was made about a product in development, a tiny 1.8-inch hard drive. But they hadn't found any market for it yet. Did Rubinstein-san think he might find a use for it?

That miniscule drive, Ruby had learned, would hold five gigabytes of data. At the time, that was simply amazing. Apple now signed an ex-clusive deal with Toshiba for the hard drive.

Miniature batteries had become available that would power the device long enough that the user wouldn't have to plug it back in after listening to what might seem like just a few songs.

And one more crucial element, as well—a piece of technology that few people would be aware of but all would celebrate. With existing MP3 players, it took hours to download your music library; the "FireWire" technology that Apple had played a leadership role in developing now made it possible to download in minutes. Together these elements would make the creation of a small, elegant iPod a reality.

Apple's software expertise could create a dramatically superior portable music device. Plus the company had great industrial design chops and a genius for miniaturization.

"So Steve asked me to go do a music player," Ruby said.

Imagine working on a product so desirable that the members of the development team can hardly wait to finish it so they could each have one of their own. That's what happened with what came to be called the iPod. The idea of being able to carry a big part of your music library around with you was irresistible.

As Jonathon Ive described it, "Like everyone else on the project, I knocked myself out, not so much because it was a challenge—which it was—but because I wanted to have one." And, "I cannot remember the last time where we were collectively lusting after a product as badly as after an iPod."

But Steve had demanded that the product be ready to launch so it could be sold during the Christmas shopping season in 2001. That gave the iPod teams only around ten months to make the iPod happen, a unbelievably short timetable.

The design challenge for Apple was to achieve vastly better performance while shrinking the circuitry into a package not much bigger than the size of a pack of cigarettes.

Getting the basic concepts into place didn't take long, but then Apple needed someone to help with the design. According to one team member who was close to the action, Ruby called around. One likely candidate had just taken a job elsewhere, but suggested Ruby talk to Tony Fadell. Ruby made some calls, tracking him down in the middle of a ski trip. He came in for a conversation. Tony would say later that Ruby wouldn't tell him what he would be working on, but hired him, initially as a consultant.

Like all Apple projects, the key players continually brainstormed about how to put it all together—Steve, Ruby, Jeff Robbins, and Phil Schiller.

But of course Steve wasn't the passive exec sitting in his office and waiting for the team to show up with a finished product. As you would expect from what you've read of him in these pages, his involvement in the iPod's development was close and constant. He drove the team with his instinctive grasp of the marketing necessities and his demand for dazzling design. He brought to the project his career-long insistence that products be remarkably easy to operate. He would grump if it took three pushes of the button to get the song he wanted, fume if the menu didn't show up fast enough, and become demanding if the music fidelity wasn't outstanding.

Although the project was tracking on schedule, late in the iPod's development, the group discovered a potentially fatal defect. The device drew power from the battery even when turned off. Three hours after a charge, the battery power would be exhausted. The discovery came when the electronic circuitry had been declared finished and assembly lines were being set up. It took weeks to figure out how to fix the problem. One of the key players from an outside company recalled, "For eight weeks they thought they had a three-hour MP3 player."

The Challenge of Timing

A series of external events cast shadows over the upcoming iPod launch. In late October, Intel cast a pall by announcing that it was getting out of the consumer electronics business. Intel was renowned for its engineering brilliance and marketing savvy . . . yet it was now admitting that it couldn't figure out how to make money in consumer electronics. And one of the division's products had been a portable MP3 player.

The Intel decision had come on the heels of other legal and economic concerns. The "dot-com bubble" had burst, leaving the high-tech industry littered with the rubble of failed companies and an army of walking-wounded out-of-work engineers. On top of all that, lawsuits about music copyright infringement and failure to pay royalties were congesting court dockets.

Worst of all, this was 2001. The tragic September 11 terrorist attacks on the World Trade Center came just a month before the scheduled launch of the iPod. Americans were stunned, horrified, and frightened about what such an event might mean for America. The people of a nation in mourning were worrying about whether some equally devastating follow-up attacks were already developed and ready to launch.

All the plans had been laid for a high-profile iPod introduction hardly more than a month later. Steve was faced with the decision of whether to go ahead as planned with the debut of his groovy little music player.

Yet nothing is as heartwarming as a birth announcement. The world might have felt as if it were falling apart, but Steve Jobs held to his plans.

Being an Evangelist for Your Product

In the Stevian tradition, at Apple headquarters, on October 23, Steve stepped before the invitation-only audience and offered the world his beautiful new offspring, the iPod, a Fred Astaire tap dance of nimble technology.

Soon Apple's innovators and Steve himself would see their ultra-cool white earphones being worn around the world by people tapping their feet.

Steve Jobs had led his teams to set a new standard for innovation and evangelized the Whole-Product team—not just the internal folks but the external ones, too.

As well as I knew him, his performances in launching a product always brought the movie *Elmer Gantry* to mind, with Burt Lancaster playing the role of a hellfire-and-brimstone evangelist out to enthrall the faithful and convert the doubters. Steve Jobs, a master at enthralling the Apple faithful and converting any doubter, is the *ultimate* product evangelist.

Persuading and Engaging in Wider Circles

When the circumstances call for it, Steve is just as much of an evangelizing showman in one-on-one or one-on-a-few situations. His negotiations with the major players in the music industry, crucial to making the iTunes Music Store possible, provide another case study in evangelizing innovation and seeing the Whole Product as a total experience. Steve's complete identification with the customer meant that he saw every piece of the iTunes Music Store experience, from its creation, to its sales, to its use, to its everyday pleasure—all of this as part of an entire system.

At the time, music profits were plummeting, dipping an alarming 8.2 percent in 2002 alone. The five major record companies and their trade association, the Recording Industry Association of America (RIAA), blamed the decline on the piracy made possible by Napster and its kin.

The RIAA went to court and got Napster shut down, but other file-sharing services such as KaZaA, which operated on a distributed model with no central server, were proving harder to eliminate. The RIAA's legal actions against both individual and organizational lawbreakers were also proving a public-relations disaster that did anything but endear the music business to the fans: their customers.

Meanwhile, industry bigwigs were trying to create their own online music distribution systems. Three of the big five record companies, Time Warner, EMI, and Bertelsmann, launched one venture, Music Net, while the other two, Sony and Universal, came up with the competitive Pressplay. Each group foolishly refused to allow the other's music on its network. They also made the fundamental mistake of charging monthly subscription fees that effectively meant customers never really owned the music they had accessed: Cancel your subscription and the music you had already paid to download to your computer wouldn't play any longer!

Downloading music onto portable MP3 players was also frowned on. MusicNet made this impossible at first, and Pressplay's restrictive policies weren't much better. By the time the two competing systems decided to license music to one another, it was too late. Download restrictions were loosened up somewhat, but not nearly enough, and fans were more disenchanted than ever. The recording industry was making the most fundamental business mistake possible: ignoring the customer's needs.

People in the music business would have laughed if you had said someone from the high-tech world might emerge as their white knight. After all, computers and the web were the enemies that were destroying their livelihood. Any other tech guru would have probably failed to overcome this resistance, but Steve was Steve, and being Steve he was not only right but persistent.

He and his cohorts at Apple insisted that the issue of music piracy was fundamentally behavioral, not technological, as the music industry believed. It wasn't the technology that was to blame, but how people were using it. Besides, the technology was not going to go away, and hoping it might be lassoed under control was worse than wishful thinking—it was harmful.

As *BusinessWeek* reporter Alex Salkever wrote in an April 2003 piece, "All along, Steve has espoused an approach that makes buying music online easier rather than one that tries to make pirating it harder." A 2003 federal court decision that peer-to-peer file-sharing services had legitimate uses quite apart from music piracy also appeared to support Steve's "behavior, not technology" argument.

Very simply, Steve saw that trying to quash the "enemy"—all those people illegally downloading music—was futile, a waste of time, doomed to failure, and likely to lead the recording industry to condemn itself to implode.

Reasoned arguments had previously done little to overcome record industry hostility. There was no question that the new technology was extremely disruptive and had all but destroyed the established financial models of the music business.

Steve told the recording industry that survival was possible, but only if it was truly open to trying something new. Nothing stays the same in business, and the only way to meet innovation is with more innovation.

That he wasn't coming from a position of strength didn't deter Steve a bit. At that point, Apple's market share was still only 3 percent, and as Hilary Rosen, who headed the RIAA at the time, put it with considerable frankness, "Apple had such a small market share that it made [the record companies'] risk fairly low."

The experience of the industry leaders had shown them that people from the technology world had little understanding of the music industry, its structure, or its financial basis. Steve was different. He had done his homework and came with a thorough insider's understanding, thanks to his remarkably quick grasp of business essentials. It also didn't hurt that Steve could pick up the telephone and ask questions of star musicians like Bono and Mick Jagger.

In the end, what carried the day? As the RIAA's Rosen described it, industry agreement came about "because of the sheer willpower of Steve. His sheer charisma and his intensity absolutely made a difference."

One EMI executive could apparently do nothing but talk about how great Steve was for weeks on end.

When the dust had settled, Steve had managed what the leaders of the industry had been unable to do among themselves: He had convinced all five major record companies to come to a single arrangement that they were all in accord with: Steve would be allowed to offer all of their music through Apple's new iTunes Music Store.

The big five also protected themselves by stipulating that the term of the first iTunes Music Store contract was to extend for only a year, unless renewed.

The music industry could relate to a businessman as obsessed with design and style as Steve, a still-young executive who had the unlikely combination of technology knowledge, a love of music, and a thorough understanding of the music industry.

Of course, the iTunes Music Store proved so wildly successful that none of the record company leaders would have dreamed of exercising the right not to renew. At the end of the year, they were lined up, pens in hand.

On Becoming Your Own Product Evangelist

Steve Jobs does not have a patent on evangelizing innovation, but as in other things, he provides us all a model. I continually check myself to see if I'm thinking in terms of the Whole-Product development—remaining open to all potential sources of ideas, inside or outside my company. As my own product evangelist, I try to approach every suggestion that might improve the product with the attitude of "Yes, we can"—the attitude that every idea is worthy of being given due consideration and not being rejected out-of-hand.

Like me, you need to remind yourself about staying open to input not just from your staff but from other people, always remaining aware that you are the evangelist for your product—evangelizing even to chance acquaintances, including people outside the industry and people who would not be potential customers for the product. I preach to all of them about my ideas. Amazing input has come from people I hardly know.

The criterion for the product itself, and every conceivable improvement, is, "Will this help the purchaser?" And the main way of answering that is, "Will I personally want this feature—will I want it and use it?" If the answer is no, that's the end of the road.

Like Steve, I grasp an idea much better when it's presented to me *visually*. I tell my people, "Bring me your ideas in model or prototype form, or in a demo I can see on the computer. Just telling me or giving me a write-up means I have to try to imagine what's in your mind. Whenever practical, I need to *see* it."

In the product-design phase, I always remind myself to think first in terms of developing the Whole Product in-house. And when that's not practical—when there are compelling reasons why some major elements need to come from outside vendors—I still need to be in charge of making certain that the product will work as well as if we had designed it all ourselves. Outside technology is okay as long as I have the control that insures the Whole Product will work as I envisioned.

PART IV

BECOMING COOL: A DIFFERENT VIEW OF SELLING

The Door Opener
Branding

Steve Jobs and Steve Wozniak started Apple in the great Silicon Valley tradition, attributed to HP founders Bill Hewlett and Dave Packard, of two guys in a garage.

It's part of the history of Silicon Valley that one day during that early garage period, Steve Jobs saw an Intel ad that used images everyone could relate to, items like hamburgers and poker chips. Technical terms and symbols were conspicuous by their absence. Steve was so impressed by the approach that he decided to find out who had conceived the ad. He wanted this magician to weave the same spell for the Apple brand, since Apple was still flying way below the radar.

Steve called Intel and asked who did their advertising and PR. He found out that the mastermind behind their ads was a man named Regis McKenna. He called McKenna's secretary for an appointment but got the brush-off. So he kept calling—and calling—upwards of four times daily, every single day. The secretary finally begged her boss to take the meeting, just to get Steve off her back.

Steve and Woz showed up in McKenna's office to deliver their pitch. McKenna listened politely and informed them he wasn't interested. Steve didn't budge. He kept telling McKenna how great Apple was going to be—every bit as big as Intel. McKenna was too polite to push him out the door and finally Steve's persistence carried the day: McKenna agreed to take Apple on as a client.

Well, it's a good story. But despite the fact that it's told in various books, it didn't really happen like that.

How it really happened, Regis says, is that he had gotten started at a time when technology ads flogged the technical details of the products. When he landed Intel as a client, he managed to get their acceptance on creating ads that were "colorful and fun." The brilliant stroke had been hiring "a creative director out of the consumer industry who couldn't tell the difference between a microchip and a potato chip," so he created ads that caught the eye, even though, for Regis, convincing the clients wasn't always easy. "It took a lot of hard selling to Andy Grove and others at Intel."

It was the kind of creativity Steve Jobs was looking for. At that first session, Woz showed Regis a paper he had written as the basis for an ad; it was filled with technical language and "he was reticent about having anyone 'rewrite' his stuff," so Regis said he didn't think he could do anything for them.

This was typical Steve—knowing what he wanted and not giving up. After the first turndown, he called and scheduled another appointment, this time without telling Woz. At their second session together, Regis formed a different impression about Steve, one that he has talked about through the years ever since: "I've often said that the only true visionary people I ever met in Silicon Valley were Bob Noyce [of Intel] and Steve Jobs. Jobs gives Woz much praise for being the engineering genius but it was Jobs who gained the confidence of the investors and continued to project and drive the vision of Apple."

Steve walked out of that second meeting with an agreement from Regis to take on Apple as a client. "Steve was and still is very persistent when he wants to achieve something. At times it was difficult for me to exit meetings with him," Regis says.

(As a side note: To raise funding for the business, Regis sent Steve to talk to venture capitalist Don Valentine, who was then General Partner at Sequoia Ventures. "Don called me afterward," Regis recalls, "and asked, 'Why did you send me these renegades from the human race?'" But Steve won him over, too. Valentine didn't want to invest in the "renegades" but passed them along to Mike Markkula, who got the company off the ground with an investment of his own that made him an equal partner with the two Steves. He also set them up with the company's first major round of financing, through investment banker Arthur Rock, and later, as we've seen, became acting CEO.)

To me, there is one more remarkable feature of this episode of Steve seeking out Regis and then convincing him to accept Apple as a client. It's that Steve, still very young and at the time far less experienced than you, the reader, probably are, somehow understood the critical value of branding. No university or grad school degree in business, no one in his growing up who was a manager or executive in the business world whom Steve might have learned from. Yet he somehow grasped from the very first that Apple could only be a major success if it became familiar as a brand.

Most business people I've known still haven't grasped that governing principle.

Steve and the Art of Branding

Picking the advertising agency to work with Regis in establishing Apple as a brand, a name everyone would know, wasn't much of a challenge.

Chiat/Day had been around since 1968 and were doing some of the most creative commercials anyone had seen. Journalist Christy Marshall nailed the agency beautifully with this description: "a place where success breeds arrogance, where enthusiasm borders on fanaticism and where intensity looks suspiciously like neurosis. It is also a bone in the throat of Madison Avenue, which derides its inventive, often riveting ads as irresponsible and ineffective—and then mimics them." (Chiat/Day, again, was the agency that produced Apple's "1984" commercial, and the journalist's description gives a clue to why Steve picked them.)

For anyone who ever needs clever, innovative advertising and has the guts to dare use an in-your-face approach, the journalist's description provides an unusual but fascinating checklist of what to look for.

The man who dreamed up "1984," Chiat/Day adman Lee Clow (who is by now the head of the global advertising conglomerate TBWA), has his own take on the care and feeding of creative people. They are, he says, "50 percent ego and 50 percent insecurity. They need to constantly be told they're good and they're loved."

When Steve finds a person or a company that meets his demanding standards, he becomes dependably loyal. Lee Clow explains that it's common for major companies to suddenly change ad agencies, even after years of stupendously successful campaigns. But with Apple, he says, the situation was very different. It's been "a very personal deal from the very beginning." Apple's attitude has always been, "As long as we succeed, you succeed. . . . When we're doing good, you're going to do good." And you only lose the account if we go out of business.

What Clow was describing is the way Steve Jobs has been loyal to his designers and creative teams from the beginning and all through the years. Clow calls that loyalty "a way of being respected for your ideas and your contribution."

• • •

Steve showed a sense of the loyalty Clow was talking about in his relationship with Chiat/Day. When Steve left Apple to start NeXT, the Apple leadership quickly dumped his choice of ad agency. One of Steve's early actions when he returned to Apple ten years later was to rehire Chiat/Day. Names and faces have changed over the years but the creativity is still there, and Steve still had that loyal respect for their ideas and contribution.

Poster Boy

Few people ever manage to become a cover girl or cover boy, their face familiar from magazine covers, newspaper articles, and television stories. Most of the people who do are, of course, politicians, sports figures, actors, or musicians. That kind of celebrity status is not something anyone in business would ever expect. For Steve, it happened without trying.

As Apple grew, Jay Chiat, the head of Chiat/Day, continued a process that had already begun on its own, promoting Steve as the "face" of Apple and its products, much as Lee Iacocca had become during the years of the Chrysler turnaround. Ever since the early days of the company, Steve—inspired, difficult, controversial Steve— has been *the* face of Apple.

In the early days when the Mac was not selling well, I told Steve the company should do commercials with him on camera, the way Lee Iacocca was doing so successfully for Chrysler. After all, Steve had appeared on so many magazine covers that he was much more recognizable than Lee had been when the Chrysler commercials began to run. Steve was turned on by the idea but was overruled by the Apple execs making the advertising decisions.

Granted, the early Macs had weaknesses, so common in most products. (Just think of first-generation almost anything from Microsoft.) Ease

of use, however, easily overshadowed the Mac's limited memory and
black-and-white screen. The already substantial following of loyal Apple
fans and creative types in the entertainment, advertising, and design
businesses gave the machine an early sales boost. The Mac then launched
the whole phenomenon of desktop publishing among amateurs as well
as professionals.

The fact that the Mac carried a "Made in the USA" label also helped.
The Mac assembly plant in Fremont was located where a General Motors plant—at one time the area's economic mainstay—was about to
be shut down. Apple became a local hero as well as a national one.

The Macintosh and the Mac brand of course created a whole new
Apple. But that luster wore off after Steve's departure, as Apple devolved
into a "me too" computer company, selling through traditional sales
channels like all the competitors, and measuring market share instead
of product innovation. The only good news was that the Macintosh
loyalists remained faithful through that difficult period.

More Building Brand

Studying Steve Jobs for lessons in the art of branding, you soon realize
he has a master craftsman's ability to create a consistent, positive product
image in the minds of his customers. He combines stick-to-itiveness
with an intuitive sense of exactly what it takes to get the public enthralled with a product. He understands that this isn't just a question
of how well the product is designed and how smoothly it works—
although these are of course critical factors—but of how it is perceived
by the user, which of course is the key to product success.

When Steve introduced the Apple II in 1976, he made well-known
television talk-show host Dick Cavett the company's first celebrity
spokesperson; Cavett had tremendous credibility among the educated
Apple II target market. By 1980, the Apple II had an 80 percent market

share, and was so strong a product that developers had created more than a thousand applications to run on it.

In fact, the overwhelming success in branding the Apple II—the glory that the press showered on Apple (as well as on Steve)—was what drove IBM to the decision that they needed to enter the PC market. They weren't exactly a newcomer to the arena: I had seen personal computer products in the IBM labs as early as 1976. But they were in the business of leasing mainframe computers to large companies and didn't understand the consumer marketplace. Having IBM as a competitor made Steve nervous at first, but IBM never figured out the things that for Steve were second nature. The first IBM PC was introduced in 1981; IBM closed down its PC business nine years later.

Meanwhile upstart Apple ascended to the hallowed ranks of the Fortune 500 in shorter time than any other company in history.

Sticking with What Works

Steve's associations with Regis McKenna and Jay Chiat gave them all tremendous opportunities for the creativity that continues to characterize the Apple brand. The "1984" splash was just the beginning. After Steve's return, Chiat/Day put innovative art director Lee Clow in charge of the Apple account. He came up with another home run in Apple's enormously popular "Think Different" campaign.

More recently, the iPod-wearing dark figures silhouetted against colorful backgrounds both in print ads and on billboards have become similarly indelible images in the public's mind.

In the advertising business, longevity is the exception rather than the norm. As Lee Clow has pointed out, Steve sets a model for loyalty: If it's working, don't mess with it. Chiat/Day, which has merged with TBWA and is now part of the OMD Worldwide advertising conglomerate, still remains Apple's agency. In fact, it has built a somewhat secretive Media

Arts Lab in its Playa Del Ray location to test innovations created especially for the Apple account.

Apple is a prime example of the rewards that come when you get the equation right: products that people truly want *and* great branding, which is the door opener for waking people up to the products.

Riding the
Retail Juggernaut

Steve was on a tear when he relaunched his ascendancy—and Apple's—after his return in 1996. With his left hand he was using his now-honed business experience to reshape the product line and trim the corporation to a survivable size, while with his right he began laying the groundwork for what a few would consider visionary and many would consider foolish: a move into retail.

He had the vision of being directly connected to the Apple customers. Steve Jobs, with no background in retail and no real knowledge of how retailing operated, was going to try to eliminate the middleman. Within weeks of his return, he began one of his riskiest projects ever.

The big computer chains and other resellers were raking off 35 to 40 percent of revenue on each Apple product they sold. Through his dealings with Disney, Steve had experienced the final link in his growing appreciation of the power of selling directly to the consumer, discovering the fire within himself as a consumer marketer.

He set a team to work on a technology approach. In November 1997—less than a year after his crowning as the new head of the company and eons ahead of the retail industry—Apple opened its online store. The incredibly short timetable was made possible largely by using software Steve had brought with him: WebObjects, a web server and application framework that had been developed at NeXT.

Soon Steve was announcing that the new Apple.com online store had received orders for $12 million *in its first month*.

Insight

The online sales represented great news, but sales through the traditional retail channel continued to be a frustration. Apple's market share for computers was stalled. One of the main problems, Steve believed, was the way the company's products were sold. The big computer chain stores didn't give Apple the best shelf space or particularly enticing displays. Then again, the chains had little sense of style under the best of circumstances and suffered from a very high turnover rate for salespeople. At the same time, most buyers were seeking the best deal and had very little brand loyalty—very similar to the situation at the time of the Mac introduction in 1984.

As we've seen with Steve's reaction to the FedEx direct-delivery idea, he had long believed he might be able increase market share significantly if Apple was able to do its own distribution and sales. He was as convinced as ever that Apple and Mac were powerful but were not being exploited properly.

The Apple II had been all about people buying a product they loved. Through the years, Mac users self-organized into an Apple cult. But the mega-stores' marketing was aimed at the lowest common denominator. So Steve decided to do what he does best: something new. Something in the iLeadership mode.

He explained his reasoning in a 2007 *Fortune* interview. "I started to get scared. . . . The company was increasingly dependent on mega-retailers—companies that had little incentive . . . to position Apple's products as anything unique." His conclusion, he said, was that "We have to do something, or we're going to be a victim of plate tectonics. . . . We have to innovate here."

Jumping into Retail

Steve made the bold decision to figure out a retail strategy for connecting directly with customers. The road promised to be bumpy.

Apple had previously tried to sell through CompUSA, where they created separate Apple departments within each store; the attempt had fallen on its face. During that same year, 2001, the Gateway chain cut the number of its stores by 10 percent, and by 2004 it would be out of business entirely. With even established players falling by the wayside, it seemed like the worst possible time to become a computer retailer, especially for a beginner.

But Steve wasn't just leaping into the void, as much as his competitors would have liked to believe that was what he would be doing. When it comes to talent hunting, Steve Jobs provides a great model for the rest of us. He took his skills as a talent magnet to the less technical but equally challenging task of creating a world-class retail team. For a start, he asked people he respected, and scouted around. The exploring led him to a man named Ron Johnson, a Harvard MBA who was then vice president of merchandising for Target. He was credited with Target's highly successful "affordable design" initiative, which began with an inexpensive but beautiful Michael Graves teapot, and soon became an integral part of the Target brand.

You understand by now that Steve is a stellar recruiter. It's just not that easy to say no to him, because he understands how to make any invitation he offers sound nearly irresistible—the iconic example being the line about selling sugar water or coming with him to change the world.

Soon Johnson was on the way to Cupertino, becoming Steve's senior vice president of merchandising, with the assignment of creating the new retail operation for Apple.

Steve's research also led him to Mickey Drexler, CEO of the Gap, who was considered the best of the best. Steve must have known from the outset that Drexler wasn't going to give up the CEO position of a $15 billion company to take a VP slot at Apple, but I can picture Steve's smile at the end of the conversation. Drexler had agreed to accept a position on the Apple board. That meant Steve would have the benefit of Drexler's advice as he moved ahead with his retailing goals.

Once again Steve Jobs had proved himself an effective and brilliant recruiter.

Applying the Prototypes Model

Johnson's challenge was to take Apple products direct to the consumer by creating an Apple retail store chain. He didn't have to look far for a model, nor did Steve want him to. They had one in their own backyard. Apple's employee store, started up in 1984 on Bandley Drive in Cupertino, had all the Apple products attractively displayed, and employee customers were welcome to try them out. It was actually more like a hands-on demo center than a traditional retail space.

This ethos would be transferred intact to the new stores. They were to be places you could play with products you would also be able to buy—without any pressure. Steve insisted on selling his products his way.

The Gap's Mickey Drexler advised Steve to build a prototype store in a warehouse before trying to design one for the outside world. That way, Apple could make its mistakes in private. And mistakes were definitely made.

Stepping inside the first prototype, Steve's heart sank. The store had products laid out by product type and category. This might make sense to an Apple employee, but it didn't make it easy for Apple customers to find what they actually wanted to buy. Over the following several months, the original prototype store was torn down and a new one built in its place.

Meanwhile Steve and his team faced the issue of where the stores would be located. Everyone who's ever owned a retail operation knows that the key factor is the same one set forth in the old real estate agent's saw about the three most important considerations in buying a house: "Location, location, and location."

The decision was made to place the first stores in high-end malls, basically the opposite of the strategy Gateway had followed. Apple has always been about lifestyle and customer identification, and the Apple Stores would build on this foundation in every way. The aim was to create a great shopping experience that could enhance and expand the sense of Apple-based community, turning it from a cult into a mass movement.

Launch Time

On May 15, 2001, at Steve's invitation, a gaggle of reporters toured the first Apple Store located in the Tysons Corner Center, in McLean, Virginia—the early locations chosen to be somewhat off the beaten path. Despite all the elaborate designing and planning, if Steve was hoping the event would come off like one of his ecstatically popular annual presentations at Macworld, he was quite disappointed. The location was hardly one of the mall's retail anchors. After trooping up to the second level and being given a peek at the store, located next to an L.L.Bean, many of the unimpressed journalists remained skeptical. For a time, it looked like their negative impressions might be right.

My initial reaction on walking in was a sense of calm excitement. The place seemed so well designed, so inviting, and so well organized that you immediately knew where to head for whatever you had come to find. Video editing in one area, digital photography in another, music products in their own section, game areas along the sides of the store. Each area was well stocked with products set out for you to try leisurely, play with, enjoy, with no one hassling you to make a decision to buy. The store people were obviously very well trained, too: A lot of care had gone into every element and I could feel it. I came away with the impression that the place should be called "Steve's store"—as a compliment. I thought, *He's gotten it right. This is not going to end up on the road to failure.*

IBM at one time had opened retail stores for the IBM PC. Big Blue, so many times larger than Apple, with so many greater resources at its disposal, obviously had not done Steve's type of research and recruiting.

I actually imagined people walking out of that first Apple store with their new iMac, iPod, or accessory, and thinking, "I should buy some Apple stock"—or "some *more* Apple stock."

A sister outlet located in another upscale mall, the Galleria, in Glendale, California, opened four days later.

For a company in software and hardware, getting into retail seemed like anything but an obvious move. Many in the business press were sure that the idea of Apple opening its own retail stores was Steve's Folly. After all, what retail experience did Steve and Apple have? None, or pretty close to it, and new retail businesses have a high failure rate—especially when started by people new to the game. This time, Steve the wunderkind had certainly bitten off more than he could chew.

BusinessWeek greeted the initiative with the headline "Sorry Steve, Here's Why Apple Stores Won't Work." A top retail consultant predicted that the operation would be forced to close down in a couple of years, with Apple absorbing considerable losses from its misguided attempt to eliminate the middleman and sell directly to the consumer.

With the Apple Stores, Steve Jobs was taking one more giant step on the path of selling directly to the consumer. It was a direction plenty of product companies had tried, most with little success. A lot of people were watching to see if Apple's esteemed leader would take a belly flop this time.

Despite the dire predictions by experts in the retail field and others, the Virginia store racked up more than seven thousand sales on its first day. And that was just the beginning.

As I write this, in the fall of 2010, Apple now has more than three hundred stores, including in China. The showcase store on Fifth Avenue in Manhattan is open twenty-four hours a day, every day of the year. And you won't be surprised to learn that design awards have been heaped on the stores.

After the early results had served as proof-of-concept, Apple Stores continued to be built in high-end malls that were more accessible. But Steve hasn't let himself be constrained by his original real-estate strategy. A number of flagship stand-alone retail spaces have been constructed in cities as diverse as New York, London, Paris, Munich, Tokyo, and Shanghai. On the other end of the spectrum, smaller "mini-stores" have been built in heavily trafficked areas such as San Francisco's Market Street, an effort to lure PC users into the Apple tribe. *I'm passing by anyway, and ducking into the store will only take a few minutes out of my day.*

It took a while, but the stores have become one of the great retail success stories of all time. In 2006, Apple's stores on average generated more than $4,000 in sales per square foot per year, about four times the equivalent figure for Best Buy and considerably better turnover than racked up by such retail icons as Tiffany and Saks just down Fifth Avenue from Apple's Manhattan flagship. Apple Stores reached the billion-dollar-a-year sales figure in their third year of operation, which was faster than any other retail operation in history. Only two years later, they did that much business *every quarter*—all before the introduction of the iPhone in 2008.

In creating the Apple Stores, and taking control of the entire value chain from product concept to manufacturing to point of sale, Steve turned Apple into the high-tech Disney—which is exactly what he was aiming for.

Designing Retail Spaces for the Customer

Design, paramount in all of Steve's products, has been just as central in the creation of the stores. Customers are enamored with just about everything associated with Apple, even if they aren't really sure why.

In terms of the stores themselves, the Apple design team collaborated with some of the world's most important architectural firms in creating dynamic, cutting-edge visual design and layout. Suppliers and contractors, even those at the top of their profession, say that they needed to raise the bar another few inches when working with Steve.

Like the original employee store, the retail stores create the sense of demo centers that also happen to sell products. And when you find something you want, you don't have to wait in line to check out. The staff all have portable credit-card readers that allow you to pay on the spot.

Everything about the Apple Stores, from the products to the shopping experience to repairs, is user-friendly. One of ex-Target executive Ron Johnson's great innovations was the Genius Bar. Even the name is genius. Johnson sent researchers out to ask people where they had received what they considered the best service experience they had ever had. Almost everyone mentioned the joys of staying in a good hotel.

A light went on in Johnson's head: What Apple Stores needed was a concierge service whose primary function was to help customers who had a problem with their Apple product—even when the problem was some dumb question with an obvious answer about how to use the device. But listen to the exchanges at a Genius Bar for a few minutes and you'll realize that to the people who work there, there *are* no dumb questions.

Do you have an Apple product that's defective? If the staff can't fix a product that hasn't been dropped or mistreated, they will more than likely take it and give you a brand new one in exchange.

Incredibly, there is no charge for the training, repairs, or replacements.

Putting the Brand in People

In 2010, of Apple's 46,000 employees, more than half work in retail. All Apple Store staff are trained to understand what the Apple brand stands for and to embrace the company's values. Salespeople are the face that any company turns toward its customers.

As Apple emphasizes in its online recruiting copy: "Whether you're leading a free workshop, teaching a One to One personal training session or giving expert technical advice at the Genius Bar, there's one thing you'll definitely see—people's faces light up when you show them something they never knew they could do. You'll get used to it, but you'll never get tired of it."

How many companies in America—or in the whole world—could honestly use a pitch like that in their recruiting?

It's a reminder that the attitude of your front-line people goes a long way to shaping the opinion that customers hold of your company.

Reinventing the Product Lines

The big consumer electronics firms of the past—think of General Electric—developed and sold hundreds, even thousands, of products.

Apple has fewer than twenty—an almost unbelievably small number
for a $30 billion company. (It amuses me to note, in addition to the rad-
ically small number of products Apple sells, the radically smaller and
smaller *size* of many of the products with each new iteration.)

Steve sees the ability to focus on a few distinctive products the
public wants as soon as they see them as a key to Apple's success. By
this point, Apple's customer base has long since outgrown the "Mac
cult" of the earlier years. Almost everybody now wants to be an Apple
customer.

By putting a new sales channel in place to sell products directly to
consumers and cut out middlemen such as Best Buy and Fry's, Steve
has basically changed the whole face of retail sales for computers, MP3
players, and phones. The computer industry is going to have a very difficult time competing. Meanwhile, every other industry is being taught
lessons in retailing.

Now Steve has created the complete direct-to-customer strategy,
and, boy, does it work. Apple is a major force online, with iTunes, and
at the Apple Stores. Little could I have suspected that Steve, the ultimate
shopper, would create the ultimate shopping experience.

Steve's retail approach also has a Trojan horse aspect, given that Apple's
products are Windows-compatible. If customers have Microsoft Exchange on their iPhone, they're already halfway to getting a Mac as
their next computer. And when you buy or upgrade an iPhone at an
Apple Store, you can sign up for service on the spot without going to
an AT&T outlet. No other carrier will do this—even AT&T doesn't
provide this service for other cell phones. It's a classic example of one-
stop shopping.

Steve controls his brand because he's able to sell so effectively as well
as develop his product line. That's the only way taking total control of
a brand can be done.

• • •

It's incredible in today's economy—with failures of household name retailers like Circuit City, Sharper Image, Mervyn's, and Gateway—that a new retailer would have overwhelming success. Selling direct to customers and building the appropriate infrastructure has been one of the most difficult challenges in the business world, and Steve has mastered it. His decision to totally control the product is key to a successful retail strategy.

Achieving the
Definition of Cool
"There's an App for That"

There is nothing more cool in the world of business than creating a product that millions of people immediately want, and many who don't have are envious of those who do.

And there is as well nothing more cool than being a person who can imagine and create a product like that.

Add one more element: creating a series of these way-cool products not as separate and isolated efforts but all part of a high-level overriding concept.

Finding an Overriding Theme

Steve's Macworld keynote speech in 2001, delivered to a live audience of thousands at the Moscone Center in San Francisco and to an untold satellite audience around the world, took me completely by surprise. He laid out a vision that would cover the next five or more years of

Apple's development, and I could see where it was leading: to a media center you could hold in your hand. Many people found the strategy a brilliant view of where the world was likely to be going. What I heard, though, was an extension of the very same vision he had expressed to me twenty years earlier after that visit to Xerox PARC.

At the time of his 2001 speech, the PC industry was slumping; the doom-and-gloom guys were shouting that the industry was heading for the edge of a cliff. The industry-wide dread, shared by the press, was that the PC was becoming obsolete while devices like MP3 players, digital cameras, PDAs, and DVD players were flying off the shelves. But while Steve's rivals from Dell and Gateway resigned themselves to this line of thinking, Steve did not.

He began his speech by painting a brief history of technology. The 1980s—the first golden age of the personal computer—he called the age of productivity. The '90s was the age of the Internet. The first decade of the twenty-first century was going to be the age of the "digital lifestyle," an era that would be driven by the explosion of digital devices: cameras, DVD players . . . and cell phones. He called it the "Digital Hub." And of course the Macintosh would be at the center—controlling, interacting with, and adding value to all the other devices. (You can see this segment of his speech by searching YouTube for "Steve Jobs introduces the Digital Hub strategy.")

Steve recognized that only a PC was smart enough to run complex applications, that its large screen provided a broad canvas for users, and its cheap data storage far surpassed what any of these devices could offer on their own. And he was transparent about Apple's road map.

Any of his competitors could have emulated this blueprint. No one did, which gave Apple a lead for years: Mac as a Digital Hub—the nucleus of the cell, a powerful computer able to integrate the range of devices from television sets to phones so that they became a seamless part of our everyday lives.

Steve wasn't the only person to have used the term "digital lifestyle." Around that same time, Bill Gates was talking about digital lifestyle, but without suggesting that he had any sense of where it was heading or what to do with it. It was Steve's absolute belief that if it could be imagined, it could be built. He would align the next years of Apple around this vision.

Wearing Two Hats

Is it possible to be captain of one team and player on another at the same time? In 2006, the Walt Disney Co. bought Pixar. Steve Jobs became a Disney board member and received half of the $7.6 billion purchase price, much of it in the form of Disney shares, enough to make him the largest shareholder of the company.

Once again Steve proved the standard-bearer for showing what's possible. Many thought his dedication to Apple would mean that he would be an invisible presence at Disney. Instead, while he pushed ahead with development of future eye-opening products still under wraps, he was as excited as a kid opening presents on Christmas morning about developing new Disney-Apple projects. "We've been talking about a lot of things," he told *BusinessWeek* not long after the deal was announced. "It's going to be a pretty exciting world looking ahead over the next five years."

Changing Direction:
Expensive but Sometimes Necessary

As Steve was thinking about the stepping stones to the Digital Hub, he began to notice that everywhere he looked people were juggling all their new handhelds. Some people were loaded down with a cell phone in one pocket or holster, a PDA in another, and maybe an iPod as well. And almost every one of those devices was a winner in the "ugly" category. Besides, you practically had to sign up for a night course at the local college to learn how to use them. Hardly anybody had mastered more than the most basic, most needed functions.

He might not have known how the Digital Hub, through the power of the Mac, could fuel the phone or our digital lifestyle, but he knew that person-to-person contact was an essential piece. There was such a product right in front of him, everywhere he looked, that screamed for innovation. The market was vast and he saw that the potential was worldwide and limitless. One thing Steve Jobs loves, *loves*, is taking on a product category and coming out with a new entry that blows away the competition. And that's what we saw him doing now.

Even better, this was a product category ripe for innovation. Sure, cell phones had come a long way from the early models. Elvis Presley had an early one that was packed into a briefcase, and so heavy that he had one staff person who did nothing but follow him toting the case. When cell phones got down to the size of a man's shoe, that seemed like a huge advance, but you still practically needed two hands to hold it to your ear. They really began to sell like crazy when they finally became small enough to fit into your pocket or purse.

The manufacturers had done a great job in taking advantage of more powerful memory chips, better antennas, and so on, yet they tripped all over themselves in figuring out the user interface. Too many control buttons, in some cases with none of them labeled. Lots of features that no one ever figured out how to use.

And they were klutzy, but Steve loves klutzy. It gives him something to be better than. If everybody hates some type of product, that spells opportunity for every Steve out there.

Overcoming Bad Decisions

The decision to do a cell phone may have been easy but the project wouldn't be. Palm had already made an early grab at the market with its groovy Treo 600, marrying BlackBerry and cell phone. Early adopters had snatched them up.

To shortcut the timetable for getting the product into the market, he stumbled badly in his first stab. His choice seemed sensible enough, but it violated his own principle that I've referred to as the Whole-Product Theory: Instead of maintaining control of all aspects of the project, he abided by the established rules of the cell phone playing field. Apple would stick with providing the software for downloading music from the iTunes Store, while Motorola created the hardware and loaded the operating system software.

What came out of this witch's brew was a combined cell phone–music player with the ill-begotten name of "ROKR." Steve held his distaste in check when he introduced it in 2005 as "an iPod Shuffle on your phone." But he already knew: The ROKR was a croaker, all but dead on arrival as far as even the most ardent Steve fans were concerned. *Wired* magazine poked fun with the quip that the "design screams, 'A committee made me,'" in an issue that had emblazoned across the cover, "You Call This the Phone of the Future?"

Worse, the ROKR was ugly—an especially bitter pill for a man who cared so much about beautiful design.

But he had a card up his sleeve. He had known early on that the ROKR was going to be a dog. Months before the introduction, he had called together his trio of team leaders, Ruby, Jonathan, and Avie, and told them they had a new assignment: Build me a cell phone—from scratch.

Meanwhile Steve set to work on the other essential half of the equation, finding a cell phone provider to partner with.

To Lead, Rewrite the Rules

How do you get companies to let you rewrite the rules of their industry, when those rules are chiseled in granite?

Since the early days of the cell phone industry, the carriers had been calling the shots. With hordes of people buying cell phones and pouring a huge and growing stream of cash to the carriers every month, the carriers were in position to decide the rules of the game. Buying phones from the manufacturers and discounting them to customers was a way of locking the buyer in, typically with a two-year contract. Providers like Nextel, Sprint, and Cingular were making so much money on minutes that they could afford to subsidize the cost of the phones, which meant they were in the driver's seat, able to dictate to the manufacturers what features the phones would offer and how they would work.

Then along came this gonzo Steve Jobs, sitting down with executives of various cell phone companies. Sometimes dealing with Steve means being patient while he tells you everything he thinks is wrong with your company or your industry.

He made the rounds of the companies, telling their top people, in effect, that they were selling commodities and were in the dark about how people relate to their music, their computer, and their entertainment. But not Apple. Apple understands. And then he would announce how Apple was going to enter their market but under a new set of rules—*Steve's* rules. Most of the execs weren't interested. They weren't going to let anybody shake their cart, not even Steve Jobs. One after another, they politely told him to take a walk.

By the Christmas holiday season 2004—with the ROKR introduction still months ahead—he had not yet found a cell phone service provider willing to make a deal on his terms. Two months later, in February, Steve flew to New York and met with executives of Cingular (later bought by AT&T) in a suite of a Manhattan hotel. He treated them to a full Jobsian bench press. The Apple phone would be light-years ahead of any other cell phone, he told them. If he couldn't get the deal he wanted, Apple would go into competition with them, contracting to buy wireless minutes in bulk and provide carrier service directly to consumers—just as a few of the smaller companies were already doing. (Note that he never goes to a presentation or meeting with a PowerPoint presentation or a stack of thick explanatory handouts, not even with a sheaf of notes. He has all the facts in his head, and, just as at Macworld or a product introduction, he's all the more persuasive because he keeps everyone fully focused on what he's saying.)

Cingular bit. They made a deal that put the phone manufacturer—Steve—in charge, dictating the terms of the agreement. Cingular would look as if it had "given away the store" unless Apple sold a huge number of the phones, bringing tons of new customers piling up monthly minutes for Cingular. It was clearly a huge gamble. Steve's confidence and persuasiveness had won the day yet again.

The idea of forming a separate team, kept isolated from the distractions and interferences of the rest of the company, worked so well for the Macintosh that Steve would continue to use the same approach for all his later important products. When the iPhone was being developed, he was highly concerned about security—making certain that competitors would not get advance knowledge about any aspect of the design or technology. So he took the idea of isolation to an extreme: Each team working on an aspect of the iPhone was walled off from the others.

It sounds excessive, it sounds impractical, but that's what he did. People working on the antennas didn't know what control buttons the phone would have. People working on the materials that would be used for the screen and enclosure didn't have access to any details of the software, user interface, screen icons, and so on. And that's the way it was across the board: You only knew what you needed to get your own piece created.

By the Christmas holiday season 2005, the team working on the iPhone faced the challenge of their careers. The product wasn't nearly ready but Steve had already set a target date for release, and it was four months away. Everyone was so way-more-than tired, so overstressed, that angers flared, with screaming attacks echoing down the hallways. People buckled under the pressure, quit, went home and caught up on their sleep, then stumbled back a few days later and picked up where they had left off.

With time getting short, Steve called for a full-blown demo.

It did not go well. The prototype simply didn't work. Calls were dropped, the battery wouldn't charge properly, the applications were so buggy that they seemed half-finished. Steve's reaction was tempered and calm. The team was used to his getting up a head of steam, but this time he didn't. They knew they had let him down, failed to meet his expectations; they walked out feeling they deserved an explosion that hadn't happened, and that somehow seemed almost worse. They knew what they had to do.

Only weeks later, with Macworld around the corner and the planned iPhone introduction only weeks away, and with rumors of the secret new product swirling through the blogosphere and web, Steve flew to Las Vegas to show off a prototype to AT&T Wireless, Apple's new partner for the iPhone after Cingular was bought out by the telephone giant.

Miraculously, he was able to show the team from AT&T a snazzy, beautifully working iPhone with its gleaming glass screen and its bevy of sexy applications. This was way more than a phone, it was just what he had promised: the equivalent of a computer, in the palm of your hand. Steve later said that the senior AT&T guy, Ralph de la Vega, pronounced it "the best device I have ever seen."

The deal Steve had hammered out with AT&T made some of their own executives nervous. He had pummeled them into spending several million to develop "Visual Voicemail." He had demanded that they completely revamp the annoyingly cumbersome process a customer had to go through to sign up for service and a new phone, replacing it with a much swifter in-and-out-again process. The revenue stream was even more chancy. AT&T would fork over more than two hundred dollars every time a new customer signed up for a two-year iPhone contract, plus ten dollars *per month* into Apple's coffers for every iPhone customer.

It was standard practice in the wireless industry that each cell phone bear the name not just of the manufacturer but also the name of the service provider. Just as with Canon and the LaserWriter years earlier, Steve wasn't having that; the AT&T logo was banished from the iPhone design. The company, a hundred-pound gorilla in the wireless business, had swallowed hard over that one, but, like Canon, had agreed.

This wasn't as lopsided as it sounds, when you remember that Steve was willing to give AT&T a lock on the iPhone market, the exclusive right to sell the Apple phone for five years, until the end of 2010.

Still, it's likely that heads would have rolled if the iPhone turned out to be a bomb: The cost to AT&T would have been enormous, big enough to call for some creative explaining to their investors.

For the iPhone, Steve had opened the doors wider than they had ever been at Apple to outside suppliers, as a way of getting new technology into Apple products more swiftly. In fact, the company that signed up to manufacture the iPhone admitted that they agreed to charge Apple less than it cost them, counting on the volume to become so large in time that their per-unit cost would drop enough to show a handsome profit. Again a company was willing to gamble on the success of a Steve Jobs project. The sales volume of iPhones I'm sure turned out to be vastly higher than they could ever have guessed or hoped for.

Early in January 2007, some six years after the introduction of the iPod, the audience at San Francisco's Moscone Center heard James Taylor's supercharged rendition of "I Feel Good." Then Steve walked onto the stage to a roar of cheering and applause, and said, "We're going to make some history today."

That was his lead-in to introducing the iPhone to the world.

Ruby and Avie and their teams, working to Steve's usual intense focus on even the smallest details, had created what is probably the most iconic and desired product in history. In the first three months on the market, the iPhone sold nearly 1.5 million units. No matter that so many people complained about dropped calls and no signal; again, that was the fault of the spotty network coverage of AT&T.

By mid-2010, Apple had sold an incredible 50 million iPhones.

Steve walked off the stage at that Macworld already knowing what his next big announcement would be. The fire in his belly, his vision for the next great thing from Apple, was for something that would be totally unexpected: a tablet PC. When the idea of doing a tablet was first pitched to Steve, he immediately got it and knew he was going to create one.

Here's a surprise: the iPad was actually conceived before the iPhone and had been in development for years . . . but the technology wasn't ready. Batteries weren't available to run such a large device for hours at a time. Processing power was too limited for searching the Internet or playing a movie.

One of his close associates and dedicated admirers says, "One of the things that's great about Apple and about Steve is that until the technology is ready, he won't ship the product. And that's one of the things you've really got to admire him for."

But when the time came, it was clear to everyone involved that this would be unlike any other tablet computer. It was going to have all the features of the iPhone, but more. As usual, Apple would be creating a new category: the handheld media center with an app store.

• • •

Yet, really, what was it he saw in the iPad? When the time came to sit down with the Chiat/Day concept team for presenting the product to the market, he said he knew it was going to be another product that people would clamor for—another "must have"—but he had no idea how to tell the story.

Another insider says, "We never figured the iPad or even the iPod was a sure success. We had no idea they could be this big. We just thought they were cool and we all knew we wanted one."

He also said that nobody knows what these products might evolve into. "In ten years, everyone is going to be using mobile devices. We may not even be using computers any more."

When Others Flock in Ways that Help You Make Money

When a company that makes airplanes, cars, or tractors is successful, dozens of supplier companies riding on its coattails are successful as well. The same is true for virtually every product—hardly anything is produced without parts or ingredients made by others.

To make the best quality products and become a leader in your market, you need to entice the best suppliers to work with you. That's what Steve achieved with developers of applications for the iPhone, but magnified 100,000-fold. Sure, probably 80 or 90 percent of iPhone apps are of limited interest, likely to go unnoticed in the mad bustle for attention. But look at the outpouring: At this writing, new apps are flooding onto the web and the Apple Store at the rate of *300 a day,* with more than 200,000 to choose from. And incredibly, as you probably know, most of these apps are coming from tiny start-up companies or from individuals who never imagined they would have any kind of product on the market.

Over three years, iPhone apps became a $3 billion dollar industry. Incredible!

And of course iPhone apps are coming from Windows developers, as well.

As you may know, writing an app for the iPhone doesn't require a master's degree in computer science. In the Microsoft days, apps were created only by developer companies, under license from the Bill Gates folks in Redmond. But Apple has created programming aids making the process so uncomplicated that almost anybody who isn't intimidated by computers can create an iPhone app.

I got caught up in all of this myself, almost by accident. A friend who had had a stroke subscribed to a panic-button service—very expensive and of course it was only usable when he was at home and even then was only of value if, in an emergency, he could make his way to the device and push the button. That set me to thinking of a mobile-distress app for the iPhone—a device that can always be with you.

About that time, a college student who was attending a lecture of mine on entrepreneurship approached me with an idea. He wanted me to look at an app he had written to create a panic button for the iPhone. We joined forces.

Our iPhone app, vSOS, can be programmed so that when triggered from the phone, it can send a help message to 911, to a call center, to your doctor, to family members, or any combination of those. With GPS, it can notify everyone exactly where you are. vSOS can also be programmed to transmit stills and video of your situation—an enormous asset in case of an auto accident, a fire in your home or apartment, and so on. And for the elderly or infirm who cannot afford the thirty or forty dollars a month for a panic-button service, the small fee for the app can bring a renewed sense of security.

Even the kids and twenty-somethings are application developers these days.

Another Stepping Stone to Fame

Since I was a youngster, I've thought that someone whose quote made it into *Bartlett's* or whose new word or phrase made into *Merriam-Webster*, like "catch-22," had reached a kind of legendary status.

Steve did that without even noticing. When the iPhone was nearing release and applications were pouring in from developers, he kept dropping into conversations with the team, "There's an app for that." Soon the whole team was using the line. Then it was used in an Apple commercial. And then—yes: *The Yale Book of Quotations*, no less, listed the phrase as one of the ten most notable quotes of 2009.

Meanwhile the iPhone had become so iconic almost overnight that many other companies began producing ads showing someone using an iPhone as a way of saying, "Look at us! Look how cool we are!" And in the process, all that free advertising for Apple generated even greater iPhone sales.

Apple's earnings report for fiscal year 2010 stunned even the Wall Street Apple-watchers. Net sales jumped an astounding 50 percent as iPhone and iPad sales soared, led by a sales increase in the Asia-Pacific area of 160 percent.

The popularity of the iPhone in China has generated a curious illegal trade that begins each morning in Manhattan, with a line forming outside the Apple store that is sometimes a block long, a line of silent, nervous Chinese waiting for the doors to open so they can buy an iPhone at full retail price and, thanks, but no cell phone service is required. They don't need the phones to be activated because they are not going to use them. Instead they immediately sell them to a middleman who packs them in crates and ships them to mainland China, where the prestige of owning an iPhone is so great that each will sell for roughly $1,000. One more measure of the iPhone as the coolest, most iconic product ever created by man.

Few people ever write about Steve as a paragon of morality and a standard-bearer for values, which is why I was pleased and intrigued when CBS News reported on an e-mail exchange Steve had with a web writer and editor, Ryan Tate.

Tate sent Steve a message that said in part, "If Dylan was 20 today, how would he feel about your company? Would he think the iPad had the faintest thing to do with 'revolution'? Revolutions are about freedom."

It has always surprised me that Steve, busy as he always is, finds the time to respond to some of his e-mails from strangers. He shot back a response: "Yep, freedom from programs that steal your private data. Freedom from programs that trash your battery. Freedom from porn. Yep, freedom. The times they are a changin', and some traditional PC folks feel like their world is slipping away. It is."

The exchange continued, until Steve apparently decided he had had enough. Calling Tate "misinformed," he wrote: "Microsoft had (has) every right to enforce whatever rules for their platform they want. If people don't like it, they can write for another platform, which some did. Or they can buy another platform, which some did. As for us, we're just doing what we can to try and make (and preserve) the user experience we envision. You can disagree with us, but our motives are pure."

Content Is King

It's said of some people that they keep reinventing themselves. I've long seen Steve Jobs as being one of those self-reinventors, but in a different sense. It's not so much that Steve himself has changed through the years, but that his vision has changed.

The Macintosh as a computer for everyone was first-generation Steve. Everything before the iPhone and iPad was Steve as the creator of products that catch the imagination.

Today Steve's vision has been updated to focus on *content*.

Apple's competitors see the iPad as a tablet. Everybody is making a tablet, but they don't get it.

To the pundits of the industry and all the competitors, the iPad may look like a tablet. In Steve's vision, though, it's a media device. The iPad is a *delivery platform* . . . a device for bringing content to the user. It is also, as an extension of the iPhone, a platform for applications—with the difference that most apps on the iPad will be directed at improving how we access and use content.

Google makes money from advertising, and from offering cell phone applications, but sees itself as a vehicle for allowing others to deliver content. In contrast, Steve discovered from his Pixar and Disney experiences that content rules the world. Everywhere you look these days, people are listening to music on their iPods or watching movies on their iPads . . . and paying Apple for the privilege.

Steve has envisioned a world in which content is king. The Apple of the future will become more and more a company putting in our hands devices that deliver content.

As usual, Steve Jobs has seen the future and is making it his.

Remember that line about if you look up something-or-other in the dictionary, you'll find so-and-so's picture? If dictionaries actually included iconic pictures, there is absolutely no doubt that the definition of *cool* would be brightened by a picture of Steve Jobs. One after another, he has created such society-changing products that millions of people—not just in the United States but around the world, not just the younger generations but people of all ages—have recognized that they can douse themselves in an aura of cool by being seen with an iMac, an iPod, an iPhone, and now, an iPad.

• • •

But here's the bottom line: Steve Jobs does not have a patent on cool. It really is possible for other companies, other product managers and product designers, to create new-age products that people will crave because they are so handsome, so intuitive, so functional, so pleasing to use, and so perfectly matched to customer needs.

What product do you have or are thinking about that can be so successful even Steve Jobs would take notice?

PART V

ON BECOMING STEVIAN

In His
Footsteps

Can you really follow in the footsteps of Steve Jobs—applying the principles explained in these pages to improve your way of doing business and forever improve the products you create?

My answer is yes, and my evidence is that I've done it myself, repeatedly.

In 1987, I was invited to speak about employee entrepreneurship at a Fortune 100 CEO conference in Williamsburg. There were about a hundred participants and I was pretty intimidated because I had to follow Ted Kennedy at the podium. And because a lot of industry luminaries were in the audience.

Executives find it easy to say, "Well, all that may work at Apple, but never in my company." Even so, about a week later GE's VP of human resources got in touch. The company was developing a program to promote more employee input, and was I interested in taking part?

I went to New York to meet with the team that was building the new program, and Jack Welch came in to address the group. Welch was a very strong-willed businessman who had a reputation for a tough attitude and not listening well. I didn't see him that way. He wanted to create an environment where GE employees could feel they were part of the business, and would participate in solving its problems. The program aimed at capturing and implementing the good ideas employees had for improving the company's operations—with something more inviting and more effective than a suggestions box. In other words, give GE employees something like the experience of being pirates at a start-up.

Working with a Boston consulting firm, we created a program called "Work Out" to achieve these goals. We tested it at a GE plant in Buffalo that had a reputation for being one of the company's most bureaucratic operations.

Work Out proved to be an overwhelming success. Jack himself said, "Work Out is meant to help people stop wrestling with the boundaries, the absurdities that grow in large organizations. We're all familiar with those absurdities: too many approvals, duplication, pomposity, waste." He also said the program "turned the company upside down, so that the workers told the bosses what to do. That forever changed the way people at the company behaved."

For me, the experience was one more proof that the principles of iLeadership can be applied by people at every level, and can make a profound and lasting difference.

The experience with the GE program gave me renewed confidence that what I had learned from Steve was going to be of great value in my life. I gradually became haunted by wanting to create a company with an Apple-like environment, built around a great product idea. I had learned from Steve that you need to be continually looking for ideas that will solve problems and enhance the user's productivity. And that you have to have a vision of whether any product you're considering would help make the world better.

At one point I was working with the UCLA Medical Center on an electronic medical records and voice-recognition project that had me flying to Los Angeles every week. One day I got to my hotel and realized I had left my laptop on the plane. I hated lugging that laptop around.

Someone showed me a little gadget I had never seen before: a USB drive that would let you carry your data around with you. What a phenomenal idea! This was at a time when the 256 megabytes that the drive held was enough for most people to travel with all of their files. You could carry your entire documents folder on a flash drive instead of a laptop.

I learned from Steve always to ask, "What can be done with this technology?" Flying home two days later, I knew I had a vision for a great product—your whole desktop on a USB drive. When you stuck the drive into your computer, a program yet to be developed would take over the operating system and load the flash drive with not just your files but your complete desktop and software as well. When you plugged the flash drive into another computer, the program would show you your own desktop; all your programs and all your files would be available. When the drive was removed, the desktop would be restored back to its original state; none of the computer owner's files or operations would be any different from before you arrived.

Steve's incredible passion for his products was my model. And like Steve, I surrounded myself with enthusiastic people. Handspring CEO Donna Dubinsky referred my first developer to me—a young hacker and brilliant programmer from Brown University. He would arrive at odd hours of the day on his motorized scooter, work all night, and then sometimes not be seen or heard from for days. But I had learned from Steve how to deal with pirates, and what I saw was a very young guy who grasped all the elements it took to build a successful product. The great thing about pirates is that you can say, "I really need to see a working prototype of this product," and they will work countless hours to get that to you as soon as possible.

· · ·

The USB drives of the times were so ugly and clumsy that I decided to build my own. I actually had a friend whittle the product out of wood using my specifications, and then took the model to a manufacturer to build.

I struggled over a name for the product. A name like Apple or Sony is simple, unique, great for graphic design. I wanted a name like that—not a fancy, techie name, but one that rings, and settled on "Migo" which in pronunciation has both "me," and "go" as in "on the go." That seemed to have the right combination of simplicity and dash.

As always, there were a great many technical problems to solve. Migo had to be compatible with all operating systems and all versions of Word and Excel. It had to be secure, 100 percent reliable, and fool-proof for the user.

Even pirates need a great first mate. I went to see advertising genius Jay Chiat, the brilliantly creative cofounder of Chiat/Day, the agency that had made such a stunning contribution to Apple's branding, and he agreed to handle the branding of Migo. This was right in line with an-other of those guidelines I had learned from Steve: Seek out the very best talent and resources you can find—the *very* best—and sign them up if you possibly can. And don't forget people and resources you have used in the past or have heard highly praised.

The final product was beautiful, and completely intuitive. Prompts on the screen walked you through how to use it. There was a user's manual but you didn't need it. Again, this was something I learned from the Macintosh experience. The product won awards from *PC World*, *Newsweek*, and at the Consumer Electronics Show, for design, user interface, and even for the box it came in—giving us incredible branding and PR for very little cost.

Industry pundit Walter Mossberg of the *Wall Street Journal* wrote an article calling it a great little product for your life. That review sent

Migo's stock price from $1.50 to $6.50 in one afternoon. John Dvorak also wrote a great piece on us for *PC Magazine* and Steve Wildstrom of *BusinessWeek* followed.

What happened next was even better. It was one thing for Mossberg to write about Migo, but way better when he praised it on the air. He held it up in his fingers on his CNBC show and said "This is a great little product." I felt Steve and I were back together again, that the same energy I had had at Apple was with me.

The end of the story isn't as happy. To save money, I had gone to a low-cost provider for cases and installation boards, and half the units they produced didn't work. But there was a much bigger problem: When I started the project, a 256-megabyte flash drive cost $150. By the time Migo came out, the price of a flash drive was down to about $4 for a full gigabyte—four times the capacity. The additional cost for a flash drive with the Migo software wasn't significant if you were spending $150, but once flash drives became a commodity, with dozens of different types on the shelves to choose from, trying to get consumers to stop and figure out why the Migo cost significantly more was an uphill climb.

There was another mistake like one Steve had made at Apple. As I mentioned earlier, Lehman Brothers convinced me to bring in a seasoned management team that had run public companies. Well, fine, but they had no passion for the product. I felt as if I was back at IBM. The people were smart but were so far removed from the product that they lost sight of what was really important. All they cared about was the company share price. Here was my last lesson: If you find yourself stuck with a board or investors who don't get it, it's probably time to leave. I left Migo to innovate my next product and start another new company.

Another reminder from my experiences with Steve that the Migo experience proved: His attitude was always that, if it's a technology product, it *can* be done—which is why, when his engineers had said they couldn't build a phone without numerous buttons for all the different functions, he had insisted firmly enough and often enough, and they finally managed to do it.

Migo came out of a great passion for a great product. Steve Jobs generated that in me.

Some other Steve Jobs principles that also served me well at Migo:

Be passionate about each project you work on.

Be driven by an opportunity and create a product for it.

Always be open to talent who can help.

Do your best to make the product intuitive, so a user's manual
    isn't needed.

Be really honest with yourself about your products.

Ensure that the products represent you and your traits as a person.

Work through your people and celebrate as a unit with every
    success.

Keep innovating to get closer and closer to your ideal, your vision
    of perfection that goes beyond the currently achievable reality.

Don't listen to people who say it can't be done.

As I write this, I've just finished raising venture capital for another start-up company, Nuvel, based around a product that dramatically increases the speed and performance of the Internet by improving "last mile" connectivity, as well as the user experience for all computing and mobile devices. The Nuvel product accelerates *all* traffic over IP-based networks by up to two-hundred times.

In laymen's terms, the product compresses data on-the-fly and forces the data through a secure Nuvel-created electronic tunnel at high speed while significantly improving the performance, reliability, and security of networks.

As a later addition, I created a Nuvel app store, so we can make our products available for mobile devices like iPhones and iPads. Another lesson from Steve: Keep updating your vision and keep challenging yourself by asking, "What turns consumers on?"

Of course I'm again using principles that came from Steve. Most importantly, everyone in the organization and everyone we deal with knows that I am the Product Czar: All final decisions about the product, user interface, and all other aspects go through me.

You can bet everyone on the team knows that the user interface is critical for the product. Perhaps they accuse me of trying to sound like Steve Jobs; if they do, it doesn't bother me. The simplest possible user interface is a must, the team all knows where that view of life came from, and they are committed to making it happen.

One other thing I learned from Steve was the power of top notch PR, particularly when you do not have a lot of funds. Great PR is your best foot forward with the market.

The software guys are the same ones who worked with me on Migo. They're not just pirates and great artists. More than that, they understand my product demands and how to implement top quality software products. And they have commitment: If I need a change in the product by Monday morning, they will work all weekend if that's what it takes.

Speaking for Steve

The people who have worked most closely with Steve are the only ones in the unique position to convey the philosophy and ideas that have made him so successful, as I have tried to do in these pages. The only other person who in my view has been able to capture the essence of Steve is Apple COO Tim Cook. He offered a statement that to me provides a different but powerful expression of the attitudes Steve Jobs has fostered—the attitudes that have made Apple so great—and that I believe can be adopted and put to use by everyone:

> We're constantly focusing on innovating. We believe in the simple, not the complex. We believe that we need to own and control the primary technologies behind the products that we make, and participate only in markets where we can make a significant contribution.
>
> We believe in saying no to thousands of projects, so that we can really focus on the few that are truly important and meaningful to us. We believe in deep collaboration and cross-pollination of our groups, which allow us to innovate in a way that others cannot.
>
> And frankly, we don't settle for anything less than excellence in every group in the company, and we have the self-honesty to admit when we're wrong and the courage to change.

So my final question is: What about you? How does your product, service, job represent you? How do you align with it?

The more that what you do, what you make, what you produce matches with your deepest core as a person, the more you are going to care about it and take the great pains to demand the perfection that every product deserves. And you will take greater pains to make your customers remember it and love it.

The number-one sign of product passion is whether you yourself are an avid user. You have to be honest with yourself. If you don't care about your product, how will you be a convincing advocate? How will you convince anyone the product is something that will serve them, satisfy them, and please them?

I believe that business is a reflection of its leader, its champion. Like children who sense when someone isn't sincere, you can't fake it. You need to be passionate about the products you are creating, promoting, marketing, or selling, and that means you need to be in a company and an industry you truly care about.

Steve Jobs could not have achieved what he has without passion, a commitment to excellence, great branding, and the openness to learn from his mistakes.

We could all hardly find a better path than aiming always to follow in his footsteps.

A Letter to Steve

Dear Steve,

In these pages, I've tried to a capture the *true* Steve Jobs—not the half-truth version in all those books done by reporters or Mac people who never got to see the real you. I remember near the end of a trip to Japan when we were booked to have another "state dinner" with Sony or Canon or whoever, and I said I just couldn't face another night of sushi. So you went off, and the hotel steered me to a great tempura place. I had settled in there for about half an hour when in you walked and joined me, saying you couldn't face another formal dinner, either. I've never forgotten that evening and our conversation discussing everything from politics and the future of the world to people, life, work, and love. You were relaxed, calm, and just being yourself. It was times like that when I saw the real Steve.

I've always wondered what would have happened at Apple if you had not been thrown out in 1985. It's not cool to say, "I told you so," but I had seen the future. And as I said to you in one of our conversations, you are the game—you put the rest of the players on the sideline. You've taken Apple to glory with the second largest market capitalization of any company in the world. Yet it's not market cap that makes a company, it's the people and products that do.

You clearly learned from your experience and were able to create a new standard in corporate organizations. I firmly believe the new-age company has to be product-centric and operate every day as if it were a start-up. So the new Apple is the new standard in organizational operations. All the principles of leadership are on display at Apple, and have been since you returned. You have even managed to keep the new Apple on the same road as a start-up—a very difficult task.

I am continually asked what would happen if Steve left Apple, or as you sometimes put it, if you "got hit by a bus." I tell people that Steve Jobs is not replaceable as a charismatic, visionary leader of a consumer-product-centric company, but that Steve can be replaced by a triumvirate to carry on his legacy. Apple will have a new CEO but he, or she, will fill only one part of your role. Jonathan Ive, the modest Brit who breathed life into the designs of the iMac, iPod, iPhone, and iPad, will continue to dream up designs for products everyone wants to use and own. Phil Schiller will continue to dream up product concepts, laying the path for the future of technology. One of several contenders will take over your role as the driving force over the unsung teams who translate the visions into software, hardware components, and the other elements that bring the concepts to life. COO Timothy Cook is clearly the leading contender since he has already so successfully kept all the separate pieces functioning when you have been away.

You and I once talked about how hard it is to create products, but that it's even harder to create and maintain truly effective organizations. And harder still to do both at the same time. I believe the new type of entrepreneurial organization you have created is the cornerstone of future corporations.

We all count on your running Apple for many years to come, so I want to end by presenting you with a challenge. As you know, I'm no longer involved with Apple except as a customer, so this is advice from the sidelines.

I consider you the "king of the screen." You have put devices in our hands that have amazing information display functions and can be used by anyone. We now live in a screen society, always not far from sticking the next screen in front of our faces. So now that you have mastered giving us access to all this information, I would hope that you are already working on giving the capability to our handheld devices, our iPhones and iPads and the like, of being able to monitor our health—alerting our doctor and perhaps paramedics if there is a sudden change in condition. I would hope that your future products will not only give us access to information but be able to read or detect information through the screen—monitoring temperature, blood pressure, blood count, even detecting the quality of the air we're breathing and the water we're drinking.

Everyone can recognize the value of this on a personal basis. But in addition, with over 35 percent of our national economy devoted to healthcare, the benefits to the nation could be huge.

You are way ahead of the rest of us in so many things. Perhaps you're already working on these ideas. But if not, I hope you'll take up the challenge.

Sincerely,

Jay Elliot

You have to trust in something—
your gut, destiny, life, karma, whatever.
This approach has never let me down,
and it has made all the difference in my life.
—Steve Jobs,
commencement speech,
Stanford University, 2009

Acknowledgments

From Jay Elliot

I am very fortunate to have been associated with some of the giants of industry. My experiences were all very important to this book and I need to acknowledge leaders including T. J. Watson, Chairman and President of IBM; Intel CEO Andy Grove; Intel cofounders Gordon Moore and Bob Noyce; and of course Steve Jobs. The lessons I learned working with these leaders have been invaluable to my thinking about leadership.

I would like to thank my good friend and business colleague Kim Pettinger. Her support and encouragement to write this book, plus her insight in pulling together the first outline over countless cups of coffee, have been greatly appreciated. As a personal "coach" and my muse, many of the lessons in the book on personal growth and organizational culture have her fingerprints on them. It is not easy to stand up to a tall, very experienced man and say, "You need to consider a different approach." Over the years, Kim did just that, and I hope I can support her equally in the future.

There have been many people and partners along the way whom I would like to thank. One of those is Greg Osborn, of Middlebury Group; his support of my ideas, his understanding of the passion I have for my products and of my leadership skills has been important in raising capital for my companies. Greg really understands these key attributes and has supported me in my business and contributed to getting this book finalized.

Insight into Steve's personal media needs and encouragement to do the book also came from Wilson Nicholls, my brother-in-law. When Wilson owned a video store, Steve was one of his biggest clients. Prior to Wilson's passing, we spent countless hours discussing Steve's passion for movies and how that related to his business success. Wilson used to say, "Jay, you need to write a book about this." Well, Wilson, I did, and your encouragement is greatly appreciated.

Literary agent Bill Gladstone played a major role in getting this project from concept to print. Bill and I discussed this idea many years ago but it was not until I spoke at a conference and used an outline of the book, with overwhelming success, that I reconnected with Bill. Not only did he get very excited about the book's potential, but he introduced me to Bill Simon. An excellent writer and great writing partner, Bill took what could have turned into just another business book and breathed life and excitement into it. My thanks to both Bills.

From Bill Simon

First and foremost, I want to express my appreciation to Jay Elliot, who provided a fascinating story and proved to be an admirable writing partner. Jay, I would gladly do another book with you any time.

The two of us were fortunate to have the insightful Janet Goldstein, provided by publisher Roger Cooper, working with us throughout the writing of the manuscript. She contributed on every level to making this book what it is. And, for me, it was a special pleasure to be able to work with Roger again—in particular because my last book with him was a *New York Times* bestseller.

The other member of my primary team has been Charlotte Schwartz, whose care, concern, and support have been so crucial through the long writing days. Charlotte, I hope I have been successful in letting you know how much your attentions mean to me.

My involvement in this project only came about thanks to Bill Gladstone, a literary agent without peer. Bill, I'm always reluctant to give you appropriate praise in Acknowledgments for fear you will be totally deluged by authors insufficiently represented. I do wonder, though, how many authors have been represented by the same agent, and kept busy by them, for twenty-five years!

My grandchildren Elena and Vincent are now old enough that I was able to share stories of the writing experience through the process. And thank you, Skype, for making their happy faces visible to me.

Jay and I were fortunate to have the support of a team of helpers. A tip of the hat and a thanks to: Dan Gerstein, Bill Dunne, Steve Flax, Howard Green, Kenneth Kale, and especially to Tom Lane.

I have acknowledged by name in the text numerous people who provided input for the book, but I would like in particular to express my appreciation to Gil Amelio, Steve Wozniak, John Sculley, Del Yocam, Donna Dubinsky, Alex Fielding, Bill Adams, Burt Cummings, Ian Maddox, Wayne Meretsky, Winston Hendrickson, and to all the others who spoke on condition of anonymity—for reasons that many will understand.

Finally, those of you who know me will understand what a loss it is not to have Arynne close by as I toil on a book manuscript. Though she can no longer be an active part of my life, she always and forever has a place in my heart.

Notes

Chapter 3   *Teaming: "Pirates! Not the Navy"*
44   **One engineer remembers:** Confidential source.
44   **"you need a competent tyrant":** Peter Elkind, "The Trouble with Steve Jobs," *Fortune*, March 5, 2008.

Chapter 4   *Tapping Talent*
60   **Susan remembered Steve:** Ken Aaron, "Behind the Music," *Cornell Engineering Magazine*, Fall 2005.
69   **"a very different model of doing business":** Ibid.

Chapter 5   *Rewards for the Pirates*
78   **"the greatest thing possible, or even a little greater":** Andy Hertzfeld, "Signing Party," Folklore.org, February 1982. http: www.folklore.org/StoryView.py?project=Macintosh&story= Signing_Party.txt&characters=Mike%20Boich&sortOrder=Sort% 20by%20Date&detail=medium.
82   **"Apple is a rare breed of company":** Chuq von Rospach, "Enjoying the Show, Avoiding the Flamethrower: Life Inside Apple," *Guardian*, January 2, 2009. http://www.guardian.co.uk/technology/ 2009/jan/02/apple-macworld-lookback.

Chapter 6   *The Product-Driven Organization*
91   **"for the rest of my life":** *Triumph of the Nerds.*
105   **"a growing reality gap":** Andy Hertzfeld, "The End of an Era," Folklore.org, May 1985. http://www.folklore.org/StoryView .py?project=Macintosh&story=The_End_Of_An_Era.txt& sortOrder=Sort%20by%20Date&detail=low

Chapter 7   *Maintaining Momentum*
117   **"pervasive feeling of pride, energy, and passion":** Confidential source.
120   **"prolonged and enthusiastic applause":** Philip Elmer-DeWitt, "The Love of Two Desk Lamps," *Time*, September 1, 1986.
121   **to keep the company going:** Confidential Pixar source.
124   **"a spectacular movie and a lovable movie":** Jeffrey Young and William L. Simon, *iCon: Steve Jobs—The Greatest Second Act in the History of Business* (Hoboken: John Wiley & Sons, 2005).

Chapter 8   *Recovery*

134   **"we'll both do it for fun"**: *Triumph of the Nerds*.

134   **"I was way too shy"**: Ibid.

135   **was the leading possibility:** Gil Amelio e-mail to author, November 7, 2010.

136   **turned down the deal:** Ibid.

138   **"Something's Rotten in Cupertino"**: Brent Schlender, *Fortune*, March 3, 1997.

140   **"Jobs dug into the mucky details"**: Peter Elkind, the Apple profile in "America's Most Admired Companies," *Fortune*, March 5, 2008.

Chapter 9   *Holistic Product Development*

150   **"But then it was a big hit"**: Lev Grossman, "How Apple Does It," *Time*, October 16, 2005.

157   **"Our jaws dropped when we heard that one"**: Peter Burrows and Ronald Grover, "Steve Jobs' Magic Kingdom," *BusinessWeek*, February 6, 2006.

157   **"One home run is much better than two doubles"**: Ibid.

160   **"a more collaborative, integrated way"**: Grossman, "How Apple Does It."

162   **"something like the diversity"**: Ibid.

Chapter 10   *Evangelizing Innovation*

165   **"missing an embarrassingly long list of features"**: David Pogue, "A Phone of Promise, with Flaws," *New York Times*, October 27, 2010.

170   **"What was out there was awful"**: Ken Aaron, "Behind the Music," *Cornell Engineering Magazine*, Fall 2005.

171   **"because I wanted to have one"**: Brent Schlender, "Apple's 21st-Century Walkman CEO Steve Jobs Thinks He Has Something Pretty Nifty. And If He's Right, He Might Even Spook Sony and Matsushita," *Fortune*, November 12, 2001.

171   **"we were collectively lusting after a product"**: Mike Harris, *Find Your Lightbulb* (Mankato, MN: Capstone, 2008), 60.

172   **"a three-hour MP3 player"**: Leander Kahney, "Inside Look at Birth of the iPod," *Wired*, July 21, 2004. http://www.wired.com/gadgets/mac/news/2004/07/64286.

175   **"Steve has espoused an approach"**: Alex Salkever, "Steve Jobs, Pied Piper of Online Music," *BusinessWeek*, April 30, 2003.

www.businessweek.com/technology/content/apr2003/tc2003043
0_9569_tc056.htm.

176   **"absolutely made a difference"**: Jeffrey Young and William L.
Simon, *iCon: Steve Jobs—The Greatest Second Act in the History of
Business* (Hoboken: John Wiley & Sons, 2005).

Chapter 11   *The Door Opener: Branding*

184   **"a bone in the throat"**: Christy Marshall, "Smart Guy," *Business
Month*, April 1988.

184   **"50 percent ego and 50 percent insecurity"**: Danielle Sacks,
"100 Most Creative People in Business," *Fast Company*, 2010.
http://www.fastcompany.com/100/.

184   **the way Steve Jobs has been loyal:** All of the Clow quotes: Bob
Garfield, "Lee Clow on What's Changed Since '1984'," *Ad Age*,
June 11, 2007.

Chapter 12   *Riding the Retail Juggernaut*

191   **"We have to innovate here"**: Jerry Useem, "Apple: America's
Best Retailer," *Fortune*, March 8, 2007. http://money.cnn.com/
magazines/fortune/fortune_archive/2007/03/19/8402321/index
.htm.

194   **"Sorry Steve, Here's Why Apple Stores Won't Work"**: Cliff
Edwards, "Commentary," May 21, 2001. http://www.business
week.com/magazine/content/01_21/b3733059.htm.

197   **"you'll never get tired of it"**: http://www.apple.com/jobs/
uk/retail.html.

Chapter 13   *Achieving the Definition of Cool: "There's an App for That"*

210   **"one of the things you've really got to admire"**: Confidential
source.

211   **how to tell the story:** Confidential Chiat/Day source.

211   **"no idea they could be this big"**: Confidential source.

214   **"our motives are pure"**: Charles Cooper, "Steve Jobs on 'Freedom from Porn . . .'," *CBS News*, May 15, 2010. http://www
.cbsnews.com/8301-501465_162-20005076-501465.html.

Chapter 14   *In His Footsteps*

226   **the attitudes that have made Apple so great:** Tim Cook, speaking on Apple's Earnings Call, January 21, 2009. http://www
.businessinsider.com/2009/1/apples-tim-cook-were-fine-with
out-steve-jobs.